Buyer Beware

The Crimes, Lies and Truth about Pet Food

Susan Thixton

Buyer Beware

Copyright © 2011 by Susan Thixton

ISBN 978-1453855010

Dedicated to the beloved pets that pet food has sickened or killed. And to my Sam who died because of a risky pet food preservative. You will never be forgotten.

Acknowledgments

There are too many names to list individually those that have helped this book happen. So, without mentioning specific names (I think you all know who you are) to my wonderful family and friends... For years you've patiently listened to me rattle on about pet food and supported my every effort. Thank you.

To my Internet friends... I've never met you (yet) but you are as close as family to me. Thank you for cheering me up on bad days, sending me insider information, politely correcting me when I've stepped out of line or made an error. Thank you for your unyielding support.

To Friends that have directly helped me with getting this book to publishing... Thank you so much! I couldn't have done it without you!

To those that have donated their personal stories of pet food to this book... Thank you for putting your heartaches into words.

Foreword

Expected Lifespan of our Pets

Our pets' bodies are made up of millions of cells. Throughout their lives, individual cells die and are replaced with new cells. Each cell in your pet's body is predetermined to live a particular length of time. Modern science has studied this cellular lifespan in many species of animals including dogs and cats. From this research, scientists were able to guesstimate the expected lifespan of each species. Here is their shocking estimate of the expected lifespan of dogs and cats:

**Based on cellular lifespan,
a 15 pound cat should live to be 30 years old.**

**Based on cellular lifespan,
a 30 pound dog should live to be 25 years old.**

If pet food provides all the nutrition our dogs and cats require to thrive, if pet food is as healthy as the advertisements claim it is, if science has shown a 15 pound cat should live to be 30 years old and a 30 pound dog should live to be 25 years old, then why do they die so young?

Table of Contents

Pet Food and Pet Health

VPI Pet Insurance released the top ten health claims reported in 2009. For dogs, the most common ailment was an ear infection (at an average cost of $100.00 per visit). For cats, the most common ailment was lower urinary tract disease (at an average cost of $260.00 per visit). Both of these health conditions could be directly connected to inferior pet food.

Here is the VPI Pet Insurance top ten list of the leading health conditions for which pet owners sought veterinary care for their dogs and cats during 2009.

Top medical conditions in dogs:
1. Ear infection
2. Skin allergy
3. Skin infection (hot spots)
4. Gastritis (vomiting)
5. Enteritis (diarrhea)
6. Bladder infection
7. Arthritis
8. Soft tissue trauma
9. Noncancerous tumor
10. Eye infection

Top medical conditions in cats:
1. Lower urinary tract disease
2. Gastritis (vomiting)
3. Chronic renal failure
4. Hyperthyroidism
5. Diabetes
6. Enteritis (diarrhea)
7. Skin allergy
8. Periodontitis (dental disease)
9. Ear infection
10. Eye infection

Now, here's the list again. **Highlighted** are health conditions that could easily be the result of inferior or contaminated pet food:

Top medical conditions in dogs:
1. Ear infection
2. Skin allergy
3. Skin infection (hot spots)
4. Gastritis (vomiting)
5. Enteritis (diarrhea)
6. Bladder infection
7. Arthritis
8. Soft tissue trauma
9. Noncancerous tumor
10. Eye infection

Top medical conditions in cats:
1. Lower urinary tract disease
2. Gastritis (vomiting)
3. Chronic renal failure
4. Hyperthyroidism
5. Diabetes
6. Enteritis (diarrhea)
7. Skin allergy
8. Periodontitis (dental disease)
9. Ear infection
10. Eye infection

What pet owners are not told about pet food could be making their pets very sick.

What Pet Food Could Cost You

The wrong pet food can cost you. Dr. Cathy Alinovi, DVM, provides the following conservative costs:

Sick cat or dog comes in. Pet food is suspect. Pet is vomiting and has bloody diarrhea.

$42 exam
$39.50 a day hospitalization
$117.95 CBC/chem./electrolytes
$45.00 place IV catheter
$10.60 a bag for IV fluids
$28.00 urinalysis
$21.00 shot of cerenia (anti-vomit medicine)
$8.50 tube of bio-sponge to absorb the toxins in the intestinal tract that are causing the bloody diarrhea

Day 1 = $312.55.

If the blood work indicates infection, add $21.00.
If we're thinking salmonella, add $90.00 for 5 fecal cultures.

Day 2+
$39.50 a day hospitalization
$10.60 a day for fluids
$21.00 a day for cerenia
$8.50 a day for bio-sponge
$79.50 a day (These things tend to run 5 days.)
Now, we're at: $630.95.

We probably re-checked the blood at least once. Add another $117.95.

Of course, if the cat/dog stopped eating and we had to rule out obstruction, or the blood work indicated raging infection and we needed to see where, we would have done radiographs. Two views of 10 x 12" radiographs = $94.20 and $21.20 interpretation fee.

Other things that can happen: indications of pancreatitis = $40 for another specific blood test, abdominal ultrasound (reveals information different from x-rays) = $42.

Easily, a food-related emergency can cost over $1000.00

To top it off, the patient may have long-term repercussions. It may now be in kidney failure. Depending on the size of the patient, medications may be from $20 to $60 a month.

Do's and Don'ts of Pet Food

Briefly, the following Do's and Don'ts of Pet Food will guide you to healthier pet food choices. The rest of this book will fully explain the whys of the do's and don'ts.

Just because a pet food company sponsors dog shows or donates to pet adoption doesn't guarantee they are selling high quality pet foods and treats. Here's a list of Don'ts and Do's that every pet owner should consider before they purchase any pet food or treat

Do NOT purchase a pet food with any of the following ingredients in it (and why!).

No By-products. By-products, by official AAFCO definition, are bits and pieces of slaughtered animals not suitable and/or not desirable for human consumption. By definition, this ingredient is NOT MEAT. By-products can be internal organs of slaughtered animals; internal organs such as liver, heart, tripe can provide quality nutrition to pets. The problem with this ingredient (by-products) is that it can also be a mix of all types of internal organs to intestines and these can be of varying quality. I prefer to feed a pet food with specific internal organs listed in the ingredient panel (such as chicken liver, chicken hearts) and not pet foods that contain the generic and who knows what's in there ingredient by-product.

No By-product Meal. By-product meal is slightly different than by-products because this ingredient can also include meat. However, it would most likely be meat from an animal that was rejected for use as human food because of disease, drugs, etc.

No Meat and Bone Meal. This pet food ingredient could contain any euthanized animal, expired grocery meat, used restaurant grease. The FDA determined this ingredient probable to contain pentobarbital, a lethal drug used to euthanize animals. (This ingredient in a pet food could make the food in violation of the Federal Food, Drug, and Cosmetic Act which should make it prohibited for sale.)

No Meat Meal. This pet food ingredient also could contain any euthanized animal, expired grocery meat, used restaurant grease. Again, the FDA determined this ingredient probable to contain pentobarbital, a lethal drug used to euthanize animals. 'Meat meal' is a completely different ingredient than a meat specific meal such as *"chicken meal"* or *"turkey meal"*. Specific meat meals, (chicken meal, as an example) provide quality protein. Unspecific meat meal provides protein but the quality is highly questionable. (This ingredient in a pet food could make the food in violation of the Federal Food, Drug, and Cosmetic Act which should make it prohibited for sale.) More information on meat specific meals follows in Questions to Ask.

No Animal Fat. In the cooking process (rendering) of either of the above ingredients, the fat that rises to the top during cooking becomes 'animal fat'. The FDA determined this ingredient probable to contain pentobarbital, again, a lethal drug used to euthanize animals. Specific animal fat ingredients such as 'chicken fat' are optimal. (This ingredient in a pet food could make the food in violation of the Federal Food, Drug, and Cosmetic Act which should make it prohibited for sale.)

No Animal Digest. This is similar to meat and bone meal. The FDA determined this ingredient probable to contain pentobarbital, a lethal drug used to euthanize animals. (This ingredient in a pet food could make the food in violation of the Federal Food, Drug, and Cosmetic Act which should make it prohibited for sale.)

No BHA. This is a chemical preservative linked to serious illness.

No BHT. This is a chemical preservative linked to serious illness.

No Ethoxyquin. This is a chemical preservative linked to serious illness. (More on this preservative in Questions to Ask below.)

No TBHQ. This is a chemical preservative linked to serious illness.

No Dyes. Dyes are used in some pet food/treats ONLY to please the eye of the pet food consumer. Many dyes are questioned as to their safety.

No Corn, Wheat, or Soy (or any other) Glutens. Glutens or vegetable proteins are frequently sourced from China. These vegetable proteins were the source of melamine contamination causing the deaths of thousands of pets in 2007. Vegetable glutens provide the pet little to no quality nutrition.

No Corn, Wheat or Soy in any form. Chances are any corn, wheat or soy ingredient (whole grain, flour, whatever form) is a genetically modified grain. Recent studies of three GM corn varieties fed to rats over only 90 days showed kidney and liver problems. Imagine what could happen to a pet eating a GM grain everyday for years?

No Menadione Sodium Bisulfite. This is a synthetic Vitamin K. German studies link this ingredient to serious side effects. Why use a synthetic Vitamin K when a natural source of Vitamin K is so easy to add?

No Sodium Selenite (dogs). Selenium is a necessary and required nutrient. Sodium selenite is one form of providing selenium to a pet's diet. Sodium selenite is highly toxic in large doses (should human error occur). Selenium yeast on the other hand is not considered toxic in larger doses (should human error occur). Selenium yeast has not been approved for use in cat foods. However, some manufacturers still use selenium yeast in cat food despite FDA's slow pace to approve it's use in cat foods. Look for selenium yeast in pet foods rather than feeding your pet a food with sodium selenite.

No Carregeenan in canned foods. Added to some canned pet foods and treats to bind ingredients, carregeenan is linked to cancer in recent studies.

Ok, now that you have avoided the pet foods/treats that contain risky or questionable ingredients, before you make that purchase you need a bit more information from the manufacturer. If they don't answer your questions promptly and directly, don't purchase.

Ask...
(1) Are the meat ingredients in your pet food/treat the same quality (USDA approved) as the meat found in my grocery?

(Caution: Some shifty pet food manufacturers using by-products will answer this question "Yes, our meats come from USDA approved facilities". Do you see the trick answer? Animals rejected for use in human foods come from USDA approved facilities. However, rejected meat is not USDA approved meat. Don't let them trick you.)

(2) Do all ingredients in your pet food/treat, including vitamins and minerals, originate in the United States?

(Caution: Many pet food manufacturers will respond yes if you don't specifically ask about country of origin of vitamins and minerals. Many vitamins and minerals used in pet food/treats are sourced from China. Do you really want to take the chance with Chinese vitamins and minerals?)

Almost all lamb and venison in pet food/treats is sourced from New Zealand. This is a safe country of origin.

(3) What is the shelf life of the cat food/dog food?

All pet foods have a 'best by' date stamped on the packaging. However, every pet food manufacturer varies in how long the food is considered 'best by' or shelf life. As an example, one food might have a shelf life of one year. Another might have a shelf life of three years. When you look at the 'best by' date on the packaging and it's six months in the future, one food can mean that the food was made six months ago while the other food could have been made two and a half years ago. Fresher food provides your pet with higher quality nutrition. Learn the shelf life of the pet food to know exactly how fresh the food is that you are purchasing.

(4) Who makes the foods/treats and where is (are) the plant(s) located?

Some pet foods/treats are manufactured at another pet food company's plant. The 'making' of the food is sort of sub-contracted. Other pet food manufacturers own their own manufacturing plants for dry and canned foods. A pet food company owning its own manufacturing plant does not make a pet food/treat better or worse but it is information you deserve to know.

If the pet food has a specific meat meal ingredient such as chicken meal.....

(5) Does your chicken meal (or other meat meal ingredients) contain muscle meat only or does it contain internal organs and/or bone?

A recent study from EWG.org showed a link to high levels of fluoride to bone ingredients in pet foods. High levels of fluoride is linked to bone cancer. Meat meals using muscle meat only would have lower fluoride levels.

If the pet food has fish meal or a fish oil ingredient (not a fish ingredient - fish 'meal' and any fish meal variety or fish oil)...

(6) What does your fish meal and/or fish oil supplier use as a preservative? Is it ethoxyquin? If not, what preservative is used?

Here's a perfect example of how tricky pet food can be. If the pet food manufacturer does not add an ingredient to the food, it does not have to list it on the label. So...if a fish meal supplier adds a preservative (required by law), the pet food manufacturer is not required to state that preservative on the pet food label even though it's in the food/treat. Some pet food companies insist on natural preservatives such as Naturox or mixed tocopherols while others use risky chemical preservatives such as ethoxyquin.

If the pet food is canned...

(7) Do your pet food cans contain a BPA lining?

BPA or Bisphenol A is a chemical in plastic commonly used as a liner in canned foods. Recent studies have proven a link between consumption of BPA and serious illness because the chemical leeches into the food.

Don't purchase a pet food/treat without knowing all the above information first.

Think You Can't Afford Quality Pet Food?

If you are thinking you can't afford quality pet food, here is evidence that you can...

No pet food company offers a guarantee their dog food or cat food will not be recalled (although they should – with the offer of paying your vet bills if the worst happens). Many pet food experts firmly believe providing your dog or cat a food that contains the highest quality ingredients, highest quality sources for ingredients, health promoting ingredients, and prompt, honest answers to petsumer questions to be a safer, healthier pet food that could help you avoid a pet food emergency at the vet. However, many pet owners assume they simply cannot afford to purchase a pet food that uses high quality meats and health-promoting ingredients. To dispel that myth, below you'll find a breakdown of costs for three randomly chosen dog foods and three randomly chosen cat foods on PetFoodDirect.com. And remember… *"a food-related emergency can cost over $1000.00."*

For comparison purposes, all of the foods below contain chicken ingredients. Pet foods were chosen at random as examples of three different price categories of pet foods available at PetFoodDirect.com.

Dog Foods

GoodLife Recipe Dog Food – considered a mid-price range pet food. Ingredients include corn, chicken by-products (By AAFCO definition, it is not considered human grade and includes no meat.) and animal fat, one of several ingredients the FDA determined to be the most likely pet food ingredient to contain the euthanizing drug pentobarbital and thus would be a likely pet food ingredient to contain a euthanized animal). Ingredients do not include probiotics (health promoting bacteria to strengthen the pet's immune system) or chelated minerals (chelated or proteinated minerals provide the pet easier absorption of necessary minerals). This dog food contains only one meat ingredient (chicken) according to AAFCO definitions.

Pet Food Direct price - $7.19 4 lb bag = $1.80/lb

Pedigree Dog Food – considered a low price range pet food. Ingredients include meat and bone meal (one of several ingredients the FDA determined to be the most likely pet food ingredient to contain the euthanizing drug pentobarbital and thus would be a likely pet food ingredient to contain a euthanized animal), corn gluten meal, corn, chicken by-product meal (by AAFCO definition is not considered human grade and includes no meat), animal fat with BHA/BHT (one of several ingredients the FDA determined to be the most likely pet food ingredient to contain the euthanizing drug pentobarbital and thus would be a likely pet food ingredient to contain a euthanized animal), BHA/BHT (a chemical preservative linked to serious illness.), and dyes. Ingredients do not include probiotics (health promoting bacteria to strengthen the pet's immune system) or chelated minerals (chelated or proteinated minerals provide the pet easier absorption of minerals). This dog food contains no meat ingredient according to AAFCO definitions.

Pet Food Direct price $20.33 16.3 lb bag. = $1.25/lb

Nature's Logic Dog Food – considered a high price range pet food. Ingredients include chicken meal (a dense source of meat protein), millet, chicken fat, three different animal protein ingredients, chelated minerals, probiotics, and other health-promoting ingredients such as kelp, alfalfa, and flaxseed. Ingredients do not include any chemical preservatives, by-products, or dyes.

Pet Food Direct price $11.29 4.4 lb bag = $2.56/lb

Cat Foods

GoodLife Recipe Cat Food (Dry) – considered a mid-price range pet food. Ingredients include chicken by-product meal (by AAFCO definition is not considered human grade and includes no meat), corn, corn gluten meal, and animal fat (one of several ingredients the FDA determined to be the most likely pet food ingredient to contain the euthanizing drug pentobarbital and thus would be a likely pet food ingredient to contain a euthanized animal). This pet food does not include probiotics (health-promoting bacteria to strengthen the pet's immune system) or chelated minerals (chelated or proteinated minerals provide the pet easier absorption of minerals). This cat food contains one meat ingredient according to AAFCO definitions.

Pet Food Direct price $6.99 2.7 lb bag.= $2.59/lb

Friskies Signature Blend Cat Food (Dry) – considered a low price range pet food. Ingredients include corn, corn gluten meal, chicken by-product meal (by AAFCO definition is not considered human grade and includes no meat), meat and bone meal (one of several ingredients the FDA determined to be the most likely pet food ingredient to contain the euthanizing drug pentobarbital and thus would be a likely pet food ingredient to contain a euthanized animal), and beef tallow (another one of several ingredients the FDA determined to be among the most likely pet food ingredient to contain the euthanizing drug pentobarbital and thus would be a likely pet food ingredient to contain a euthanized animal). This pet food does not include probiotics (health promoting bacteria to strengthen the pet's immune system) or chelated minerals (chelated or proteinated minerals provide the pet easier absorption of minerals). This cat food contains two fish ingredients according to AAFCO definitions. However, they are not within the first five ingredients as in the majority of pet food.

Pet Food Direct price $5.49 for a 3.15 lb bag = $1.74/lb

Nature's Logic Natural Chicken Dinner – considered a high price range pet food. Ingredients include chicken meal (dense source of meat protein), millet, chicken fat, three different animal protein ingredients, chelated minerals, probiotics, and other health-promoting ingredients such as kelp, alfalfa, and flaxseed. Ingredients do not include any chemical preservatives, by-products, or dyes.

Pet Food Direct price $10.29 for a 3.3 lb bag = $3.30/lb

Comparing the cost difference between the low-end pet foods and the high-end pet foods…

Dog Food
High end costs $1.31 more per pound. Average each pound to provide three meals equals $0.44 more per meal.

Cat Food
High end costs $2.56 more per pound. Average each pound to provide four meals equals $0.64 cents more per meal.

For less than one cup of the cheapest coffee out there a day ($0.64 cent cup of coffee?), any pet owner could divert that coffee money into pet food money potentially saving them unbelievable heartache and a huge vet bill.

Save your pet! Drink less coffee!

Pet Food Personal Experience - Magic

My Magic was a beautiful, 7 year old, standard poodle who was truly part of the family. Raised with my twin boys, she was the triplet, play mate and protector to them. Without warning, a few weeks before Thanksgiving 2006, she just stopped eating and began to waste away. Even boiled chicken wouldn't entice her. She grew weaker and weaker and three days after Thanksgiving we had to make that decision all lovers of pets must make eventually, and we let her go to The Rainbow Bridge.

A few months later, the news announced the start of the largest pet food recalls in history and in my cupboard were cans with the recalled numbers. I fed that poison to my dog! Fear, guilt and horror has led me to home cook for my pets. For three years I have lovingly made their food. I feed some raw and buy only Premium, well researched kibble to feed in the morning. I will never trust big Dog Food, again. Today, my dogs are healthy, no itchies, yeasty ears or tear stains and my 10 year old Bichon no longer limps from arthritis. My vet is even a believer now, as are all my friends. The only choice for me is Human Grade, Human Quality and Human Made by me.

Lynn F.

Pet Food Regulations

We need to begin your pet food education at the source of the problem - regulations. The pet food industry is governed by two organizations, AAFCO (American Association of Feed Control Officials) and the FDA (Food and Drug Administration).

AAFCO, while not a government agency, has been given the responsibility of defining all pet food/animal food ingredients, defining what pet food/animal food ingredients are allowed, developing labeling laws for all pet foods/animal foods, setting nutrient requirements for all pet foods/animal foods,...basically all regulations that pertain to pet foods/pet treats/animal foods have been developed by AAFCO.

Members of AAFCO are representatives of the Department of Agriculture from each state. Each year, AAFCO publishes an updated version of pet food/animal food regulations known as the "*Official Publication*". Within the AAFCO Official Publication begins the nightmare of what some pet foods can be.

AAFCO states it has no authority to issue recalls. However, each member State Department of Agriculture representative does have authority to pull pet food/treats from store shelves should any product not meet AAFCO regulations. And, it often does demand pet foods or treats be removed from store shelves. Pet food industry insiders tell me some states are "*very picky*" while others seem to ignore almost everything. This means that although there should be consistent regulation of pet foods and treats from state to state, there isn't.

The beginning of the madness of pet food starts with AAFCO regulations.

AAFCO Regulation PF7. Nutritional Adequacy
"The label of a pet food or specialty pet food which is intended for all life stages of the pet or specialty pet may include an unqualified claim, either directly or indirectly..." on pet food labels.

Did you catch the problem? A 'direct unqualified claim' is a polite way of saying a lie. When you walk into a pet store and read the labels of the hundreds of dog foods and cat foods available, please realize that just about anything written on the label can be a 'direct unqualified claim'. Words like 'Healthy' or 'Premium' or 'Optimal Health' can be direct unqualified claims, just worthless words.

The following are real examples of possible pet food direct unqualified claims...

"Pro-Active Nutrition for a Long and Healthy Life"
and
"Nutritionally Complete for Healthy Body Weight"

Although every other food industry is closely supervised by the Federal Trade Commission (Federal Trade laws state *"advertising must be truthful and non-deceptive"*), pet food manufacturers can lie directly to petsumers.

Now...can you imagine what the FTC would do to a fast food restaurant if it made the direct claim that the hamburger meal was *"Pro-Active Nutrition for a Long and Healthy Life"* or if the hamburger meal was *"Nutritionally Complete for Healthy Body Weight"*? The truth is that not only would the Federal Trade Commission come down hard on such claims made by a fast food restaurant but also every newspaper and every television station in the country would report on it. But that is not the case with pet food. No one of authority seems to mind if pet food makes direct unqualified claims and lies to petsumers.

The good news is that not all pet food manufacturers lie to pet owners. The hard part is finding who lies and who is telling the truth. Every time you begin to fall for a pet food television commercial or begin to believe company integrity is somehow linked to a pet food brand donating to animal shelters, remember...pet food regulations allow direct unqualified claims - lies.

Although you will learn more about the quality of ingredients in the FDA section, briefly there are two different classifications of meat used in pet food. One is human grade/quality which is the same quality of meat you would purchase for your family at the grocery. The other is pet grade. Pet grade meats can be human grade or they can be meat sourced from diseased animals or worse. While pet owners should be told on pet food labels what grade of meat is used in their pet food, AAFCO regulations do not allow it. Which leads me to the next pet food regulation of concern...

AAFCO Regulation PF5. Ingredients

(d)(3) *"A reference to quality or grade of the ingredient does not appear in the ingredient statement."*

AAFCO PF5 denies pet food manufacturers that use only the highest quality of ingredients from separating themselves from pet food manufacturers that use inferior, poor quality ingredients. AAFCO regulation PF5 hides the truth from pet owners.

So, again, you walk into a pet store hoping to find a safe, healthy food for your cat or dog. Every pet food label can lie to you and those that want to tell you the truth about the quality of their ingredients can't.

It's absurd.

Human Grade/Pet Grade Ingredients

It is what we pet owners want. It is what we think/assume we are buying - human grade ingredient pet food. The pictures on the label show images of fresh meat and vegetables. The name of the pet food includes human food words such as 'sirloin' or 'roasted chicken'. Of course any petsumer would assume from the pictures and the wording on the pet food that this is what is inside the bag or can of pet food. However, the truth with many pet foods is far from what the pet food name and/or the pictures imply. Pet food meat ingredients (and essentially all other ingredients) are separated by some (petsumers, critics, and some pet foods) into two categories, human grade ingredients and pet grade ingredients.

Human grade ingredients would be USDA (United States Department of Agriculture) approved cuts of meat. As you will learn later in this book, pet grade ingredients can be inferior cuts of meat, even meat or animal parts rejected for use in human foods because of disease or drug contamination (and worse!). So, when you purchase that bag of kibble or can of pet food, what are you buying - human grade ingredients or pet grade? AAFCO regulations require that, on the pet food label, no reference to grade or quality can be made. However, some pet food companies directly tell customers or potential customers their ingredients are human grade - not pet grade. What gives?

I took this question to AAFCO (American Association of Feed Control Officials) president (2010) Kent Kitade. I specifically asked, "*Are pet food companies allowed to claim 'human grade' directly to customers (petsumers) or in advertising even though they are not allowed to make such claims on the pet food/ treat label?*" His response..."*States have the authority to review such advertising for truthfulness if they deem that media advertising is a form of labeling. Still a little murky but does that help?*"

'Murky' shouldn't be an option in pet food regulations.

Next, I took the question to an experienced professional in the 'human grade claim' field, Lucy Postins of The Honest Kitchen Pet Food Company. In November 2007, The Honest Kitchen Pet Food Company won a six-month lawsuit against the Ohio Department of Agriculture. Ohio had denied Honest Kitchen the license to sell its products because its pet food label stated "*human grade*". From a press release about the lawsuit..."*The court determined that the labels were not in fact untruthful or misleading and ruled that the company had a constitutional right to make truthful statements about the human grade quality of its products on the labels.*" (1)

While almost all pet foods are manufactured in a 'pet food plant', Honest Kitchen proved its foods were manufactured in a 'human food plant' and thus was entitled to the claim "*made with 'human grade ingredients.*" The consensus regarding existing pet food regulations through years of discussion with various pet food companies and pet food experts is that even if all human grade ingredients are used in a pet food, once those ingredients enter a 'pet food plant', they become 'pet grade ingredients'.

Lucy Postins' reply to my question, "*Is it legal for pet food advertising to make the 'human grade claim'?...*" "*As far as I know, any pet product on the market would have to undergo the same scrutiny we did in demonstrating to FDA that their*" *product is truly human grade so it would be interesting to ask them (or FDA's CVM) whether they actually have."*

As pet food regulations currently stand, a manufacturer that searches high and low for the highest quality/grade of ingredients, human grade ingredients, (which, by the way, pet owners want to and deserve to know about) cannot legally make the 'human grade' claim in advertising or on product labels.

While many pet foods abide by existing (and limiting) regulations on labels and in advertising, most do not when it comes to email or phone response to pet owners. In fact, many take advantage of the lack of enforcement of the AAFCO 'no reference to grade or quality' regulation. Numerous pet food manufacturers that include clear non-human grade ingredients such as meat and bone meal and by-product meal have made the 'human grade' claim to me and my team of Secret Shoppers numerous times.

Pet owners deserve to know the grade/quality of every ingredient in their pet food/treat purchases. Quality minded pet food manufacturers deserve to establish a clear separation from companies that utilize non-human grade ingredients such as meat and bone meal or by-product meal. Since currently there is no official AAFCO definition or acceptance of the 'human grade' term, AAFCO needs to either enforce the existing regulations (no claim to grade or quality of ingredient) with all pet foods/treats OR finally develop a clear definition of the term.

FDA

FDA Compliance Policies

The FDA (Food and Drug Administration) is a division of the Health and Human Services Department. The FDA's sole task, while daunting, is to protect U.S. citizens AND protect our pets (and other animals) from unsafe foods and drugs. Congress developed the Food, Drug, and Cosmetic Act (the Act) as legal guidance for the FDA to accomplish its goal of safe food and drugs. The Act is where pet owners run across two very big problems...FDA's enforcement of the Act and Congress's supervision of the FDA.

Before discussing the actual laws that (could) effect pet food safety and the FDA's lack of enforcement, be aware of one very important concern. Congress, our elected officials in Washington, has the responsibility of overseeing the FDA. Congress is the FDA's boss. Keep that fact in mind as you read.

Federal law.

The Food, Drug, and Cosmetic Act are a series of federal laws that govern pet food and human food. In order to understand the significance of the FDA's lack of protection of pet food, you must first understand the laws. No legal degree is required. Below are direct quotes from the Food, Drug, and Cosmetic Act (2) that pertain to pet foods...bold font added...

•Section 201 (f) provides the definition of food: *"The term* **'food' means (1) articles used for food or drink for man or other animals,** *(2) chewing gum, and (3) articles used for components of any such article."*

•Section 402 Adulterated food: *"***A food shall be deemed to be adulterated** *– (a) Poisonous, unsanitary, or deleterious ingredients." (a)(5)* **"if it is, in whole or in part, the product of a diseased animal or of an animal which has died otherwise than by slaughter,"**

It is crystal clear! Per federal law, no pet food or human food is allowed to contain a poisonous, unsanitary, deleterious ingredient or be sourced from a diseased animal or animal that has died other than by slaughter. However, despite clear understanding of federal law, the FDA instructs its field representatives to ignore the above laws with pet food. They are called 'compliance policies', a nice name for blatant violations of the law. Below are direct quotes of FDA compliance policies related to pet food/animal food.

"CPG Sec. 675.400 Rendered Animal Feed Ingredients

POLICY: *No regulatory action will be considered for animal feed ingredients resulting from the ordinary rendering process of industry, including those using animals which have died otherwise than by slaughter, provided they are not otherwise in violation of the law."* (3)

The above FDA Compliance Policy is a direct violation of The Food, Drug, and Cosmetic Act.

To clarify, 'animals that have died other than by slaughter' would include livestock that have died in the field or prior to slaughter AND would include any euthanized animal. Further understanding of rendering follows in this book.

By the way, the Department of Fish and Wildlife disagrees with the FDA's standing on allowing rendered, euthanized animals (further explained later in this book), animals that have died otherwise than by slaughter, into pet food/animal food. The Department of Fish and Wildlife states: "*Rendering is not an acceptable way to dispose of a pentobarbital-tainted carcass. The drug residues are not destroyed in the rendering process so the tissues and by-products may contain poison and must not be used for animal feed.*" (4)

"*CPG Sec. 675.100 Diversion of Contaminated Food for Animal Use*

BACKGROUND: *The FDA does not object to animal feed or human food adulterated with rodent, roach, or bird excreta.*" (5)

The above FDA Compliance Policy is a direct violation of The Food, Drug, and Cosmetic Act.

"*CPG Sec. 675.200 Diversion of Adulterated Food to Acceptable Animal Feed Use*

POLICY: *Diversion requests will be handled on an ad hoc basis. The *Center* will consider the requests for diversion of food considered adulterated for human use in all situations where the diverted food will be acceptable for its intended animal food use. Such situations may include:*
*   a. *Pesticide contamination in excess of the permitted tolerance or action level.*
*   b. *Pesticide contamination where the pesticide involved is unapproved for use on a food or feed commodity.*
*   c. *Contamination by industrial chemicals.*
*   d. *Contamination by natural toxicants.*
*   e. *Contamination by filth.*
*   f. *Microbiological contamination.*

g. Over tolerance or unpermitted drug residues." (6)

The above FDA Compliance Policy is a direct violation of The Food, Drug, and Cosmetic Act.

All of the above FDA Compliance policies are in direct violation of the Federal Food, Drug, and Cosmetic Act laws. In CPG 675.200, the FDA stated, "*No single set of criteria, however, can be prepared to cover diversion requests in all possible situations.*" This is not true! The single set of criteria to cover all of these horrendous food diversions into pet food (animal food) is the Food, Drug, and Cosmetic Act. The FDA simply chooses not to enforce it with pet food/animal food. None of these 'compliance policies' should even exist. The law is the law...but not with the FDA.

In a phone conversation with two FDA representatives (Office of Surveillance and Compliance), I shared with them pet owner awareness of FDA compliance policies and pet owners being dumbfounded by these policies. I told them I make the analogy of the local police issuing a statement that, "*Should anyone from one particular neighborhood rob a bank, the police would not prosecute this individual for their illegal actions.*" I shared that, in essence, this is what the FDA tells pet food manufacturers: "*Rob the bank. We won't arrest you.*" The FDA agent told me, "*We liken it to speeding*". Although I remained composed during this phone conversation, my brain was screaming! The FDA considers its own decision to allow horrendous, illegal ingredients into pet food similar to speeding! Well...speeding is illegal. Speeding cars kill innocent victims. 'Speeding' pet food kills innocent pets.

Why does the FDA give pet food manufacturers permission to violate federal law and include horrendous ingredients in pet foods unbeknownst to pet owners? We can only assume the answer is money. The FDA has chosen to provide industry a sales/profit outlet for waste. Pet food/animal food ingredients and foods that should be destroyed are diverted into pet food/animal food providing related industries profit for their waste at the expense of pet/animal health.

Compliments of FDA compliance policies, ingredients and foods that could include pesticide contamination, contamination by industrial chemicals, contamination by filth, microbiological contamination, and/or dead, dying, disabled, or diseased (4-D) animals can be (and are) packaged, labeled, and sold as premium pet food without pet owner knowledge.

FDA Absurdities

It is downright amazing (and frustrating) to see the variety of ways the FDA interprets the Food, Drug, and Cosmetic Act. It seems Canada Dry Sparkling Green Tea Ginger Ale can't say 'enhanced with'. But pet food can include meat sourced from diseased animals. Yet another ridiculous but true FDA absurdity!

In a recent Warning Letter to 'Dr Pepper Snapple Group' (dated 8/30/2010), the FDA stated *"Your Sparkling Green Tea Ginger Ale is misbranded within the meaning of ...the Act"* (The Food, Drug, and Cosmetic Act). It was *"misbranded"* because the word 'enhanced' is on the label. Here's a quote from the FDA Warning Letter to Canada Dry...

*"Your Sparkling Green Tea Ginger Ale bears the claim, "ENHANCED WITH 200 mg OF ANTIOXIDANTS FROM GREEN TEA & VITAMIN C**" with the double asterisk referring to the statement, "* *Each 8 oz serving contains 200 mg of antioxidants from Green Tea Flavonoids and Vitamin C" on the principal display panel of the product label. In the context of this label, the term "enhanced" is an unauthorized synonym for a "more" nutrient content claim. FDA has defined the nutrient content claim "more" and its authorized synonyms in 21 CFR 101.54(e)."* (7)

It seems that Canada Dry could have used the word 'more' but not the word 'enhanced'. The word 'enhanced' violates the Food Drug and Cosmetic Act Law.

In the extreme opposite of Canada Dry, any pet food manufacturer is allowed to make *"an unqualified claim, either directly or indirectly..."* on pet food labels (AAFCO regulation PF7. Nutritional Adequacy). Any pet food manufacturer can use meat or animal products from diseased animals and animals that have been euthanized or have died prior to slaughter, a direct violation of The Act, with FDA approval. (CPG Sec. 675.400 Rendered Animal Feed Ingredients) (8)

It is so absurd, it seems unbelievable. As sickening, illegal, immoral, and unbelievable as it might be, it is true! The Food and Drug Administration, supported by the tax dollars of United States' citizens (63% of U.S. households have pets), enforces federal law to the fullest extent in one field, health claims such as the word 'enhanced' and completely ignores basic law in another, pet food and treats.

FDAAA

The FDA Amendments Act (FDAAA) was signed into law in 2007 requiring the FDA to make improvements on food safety for people and pets. The first deadline required by the Amendments Act law, requiring an Early Warning and Notification System during a pet food recall, has come and gone seemingly ignored by the FDA. If the FDA can ignore the law, where does that leave 74 million US pet owners?

On September 27, 2007 President Bush signed into law the FDA Amendments Act, known as FDAAA. Section 1002(b) of FDAAA required the FDA to develop *"Early Warning Surveillance Systems and Notification During Pet Food Recalls"*. The deadline for these pet food safety measures was clearly stated; *"Not later than 1 year after the date of the enactment of this Act, the Secretary shall establish an early warning and surveillance system to identify adulteration of the pet food supply and outbreaks of illness associated with pet food."* The deadline for this to be completed was September 27, 2008.

On May 14, 2008, four months before the deadline to complete the pet food surveillance and recall notification system, the FDA held the 5th Animal Feed Safety System Public Meeting in Gaithersburg, Maryland. One would think that during this meeting the FDA would have been feverishly working out the final details of the mandated pet food recall notification system. However, quite the opposite happened. Eight months into the one year deadline, the FDA Animal Feed Safety System meeting merely restated what needed to be accomplished and highlighted existing gaps in existing programs. (9)

Still 'working on' the mandated pet food safety reform, the FDA provided pet owners with *"Update #5"* in August 2008 (one month before the deadline). This update from the FDA brags about a few speeches given by the FDA - a 50 state meeting on food protection held in August 2008 and a reminder of a formerly discussed FDA 3rd party certification program for Food and Feeds safety. There was no mention in the FDA update regarding the upcoming deadline for a pet food surveillance system or pet food recall notification system. (10)

The 'early warning system and notification system' was finally completed in May 2010 (the Safety Reporting Portal), almost two years after the deadline required by Congress.

Conflict of Interest

ConsumerAffairs.com journalist Lisa Wade McCormick has reported that, over the last two years, the FDA has received hundreds of complaints from pet owners all linked to Nutro Pet Food. ConsumerAffairs.com obtained through the Freedom of Information Act copies of consumer complaints to the FDA regarding sick and dying pets that consumed Nutro Pet Food. The FDA confirmed to ConsumerAffairs.com that it is investigating the pet food company. (11)

Pet Food Safety Advocate/Pet Food Safety Alliance (www.pfpsa.org) has provided laboratory tests of a Nutro Cat Food testing resulting in "*toxic levels of Vitamin D*". (12)

Despite the above, there has been no recall.

Nutro Pet Food is owned by Mars, Inc.

Pet Owner 'Worried' posted a comment on TruthaboutPet-Food.com's report of Nutro lab tests alerting us that a Mars, Inc. scientist sits on the Advisory Committee Science Board to the FDA. From the FDA webpage "*Roster of the Science Board to the Food and Drug Administration*" is the following member listing...

Catherine E. Woteki, Ph.D., R.D.
Expertise: Nutrition, Food Safety
Term: 09/30/07 - 12/31/10
Global Director of Scientific Affairs

Mars, Inc.
6885 Elm Street
McLean, Virginia 22101-3883 (13)

The FDA states they try to "*recruit qualified experts with minimal conflicts of interest*" for FDA advisory committees. Why wouldn't a representative of a corporation be considered a 'conflict of interest' to an FDA advisory committee?

Pet Food Personal Experience - Blackie Jr.

My search for the truth about commercial pet food began with a tragedy that forced me to examine the choices I had been making every day with regard to care of my cats. One of those critical choices was the food I purchased and fed to them. My choices, as a consumer, ultimately led to the near death of my kitties, Blackie Jr., who became seriously ill as a direct result of the food I was feeding him.

I began this research after Blackie Jr. nearly died of uremic poisoning. One night, six years ago, my precious baby Blackie Jr. straggled in and flopped down in front of me, unable to walk. After rushing him to a local small town vet on call, the vet was able to drain is bladder through a catheter.

What I saw, that night in the vets office, was horrifying, what oozed out into the cold metal sink was a sickening mixture of blood, urine, puss and crystals that slowly drained from Blackie's lifeless body. The veterinarian informed me that he would die immediately if I did not rush Blackie to the animal hospital 75 miles away, the only one equipped to deal with serious cases like Blackie's. He hung an IV from my car window attached to Blackie with the instructions not to stop for any reason, and with that my journey began.

These are my first and feeble steps at recording for others, the epic drama of the tale of Blackie and my emergence from a loving, but clueless, caretaker of my kitties to an informed consumer.

This research is the result of my effort to help my cat Blackie Jr. to remain healthy after his near fatal illness with FUS/FLUTD. The medical costs were over $3000 and at the time of his illness I had been led to believe by the pet food industry I was feeding him the best commercial food available.

What began initially as research into Blackie's diagnosis of chronic FUS/FLUTD six years ago, ultimately led to information about the critical role pet nutrition plays in this disease.

Mollie M.

2007 Pet Food Recall

Some estimates are as high as 350,000 dogs and cats - family members - died as a result of the 2007 pet food recall. Criminals responsible were never jailed. Pet food manufacturers went on making billions while grieving pet owners struggled to pay vet bills. Four years later, money from the pet food lawsuit - won by Pet Owners against Menu Foods - has yet to be disbursed.

Melamine

March 2007 taught the world a new word, melamine. Although melamine has been around for years in the making of plastics, few consumers knew of the word or paid much attention to it. Then in March 2007 when thousands of pet owners learned that unscrupulous Chinese suppliers used melamine to boost the protein analysis of some common pet food ingredients to earn a few more dollars, melamine became a household word. After the pet food horror, melamine went silent for a few months but in 2008 it became a topic of concern all over again when it was discovered to be in everything from baby formulas, to candy, to powdered cheese – various products recalled worldwide.

The worry for US consumers is not only what product will be re-called next due to melamine contamination but also if there have been melamine contaminated products that have slipped into the US unnoticed. Currently only 1% to 3% of all foods and drugs imported into the United States are inspected by the FDA. This means that anywhere from 97% to 99% of all imported food and drugs are not inspected, including 97% to 99% of all imported potential melamine-risk products from China.

Enter into concern a new report from the National Institute of Diabetes and Digestive and Kidney Diseases dated October 8, 2008. This shocking report tells us that chronic kidney disease is up 30% in the US over the last decade. (14) This is such an increase in reports of kidney disease that for the first time in history the US Renal Data Systems published a separate report documenting *"the magnitude of the disease, which affects an estimated 27 million Americans and accounts for more than 24 percent of Medicare costs."* National Institutes of Health director Elias A. Zerhouni, MD states *"the major focus on chronic kidney disease in this year's report acknowledges that this disorder is a growing public health issue deserving of wider public awareness and intensified scientific investigation."*

A method of defense to protect your family would be country of origin ingredient information provided on every product you purchase. Unfortunately, the FDA has no plans to provide consumers with complete country of origin information. On September 30, 2008 the COOL Law – Country of Origin Labeling – was enacted requiring country of origin information for certain beef, lamb, pork, chicken, goat, veal, wild and farm-raised seafood, fresh or frozen fruits and vegetables, peanuts, pecans, macadamia nuts and ginseng sold in the United States. The COOL Law does not require any potential melamine risk products or ingredients to provide country of origin information to consumers. As the laws currently stand, consumers have no way of knowing if any ingredient in their coffee creamer, or dried cheese, or pet foods or hundreds of other potential risk items originated from China.

A recent article in the Wall Street Journal perfectly explains the dilemma for US consumers with Chinese imports. (15) While China tells the world that potential melamine-tainted products are under close scrutiny, the real story is quite different. *"A reporter at Southern Weekend magazine first blew the whistle on reports of babies possibly sickened by milk powder in late July. Or rather, he would have if he and his editor had been allowed to publish an article on the case. Instead, the story fell victim to a directive from the Propaganda Department forbidding negative reporting on food safety ahead of the Olympics. This episode shows how China's media controls make it impossible for the press to serve as an effective watchdog. Since the milk scandal erupted, Beijing has grown more restrictive, not less."*

At an International Food Safety meeting held in Taiwan on October 16, 2008, melamine was *"one of the key issues"* discussed. A U.S. FDA representative was quoted as saying *"there are no safety concerns with 2.5 ppm (parts per million) of melamine in foods."* On the contrary, the new Department of Health in Taiwan decided that food products containing dairy and non-diary ingredients must test 100% negative for melamine after melamine was found in Pizza Hut dried cheese packets in Taiwan. (16)

A 30% increase in kidney disease in the US is a startling statistic. U.S. consumers will probably never know if the increase has a connection to melamine. Regardless, the FDA needs to step forward and immediately implement changes in the COOL Law to include any and all products or ingredients of products that have the slightest potential for melamine contamination.

More Melamine

Seventy-six tons of dairy products laced with melamine were seized in China June 2010. The melamine nightmare continues.

Reports from China are alluding that this melamine discovery is left over from the 2008 melamine-tainted milk horror which killed six babies and sickened 300,000 children. From an article on CBSNews.com "*It is crucial to account for the amount that was contaminated back in 2008 and make sure it is being destroyed or disposed of safely,*" said Dr. Peter Ben Embarek, a World Health Organization senior scientist on food safety based in Beijing. "*As long as part of it is still not accounted for, or destroyed properly, we will unfortunately see these types of things happening again.*" (17)

An article from Wisconsin Ag Connection states "*Inspectors in Gansu Province first discovered contaminated samples of milk powder brought to them for testing by a worker at the Dongyuan Dairy Factory in adjacent Qinghai Province. Qinghai officials later found that 64 tons of raw dairy products and 12 tons of finished goods were tainted with melamine, some at up to 559 times the legal maximum.*

Both the factory owner, Liu Zhanfeng, 54, and the production manager, Wang Haifeng, 37, were taken into police custody, Xinhua reported. Officials said most of the contaminated material was destined for Zhejiang Province, near Shanghai." (18)

A National Toxicology Program report on melamine states there is a "*clear need for updated risk assessment*" of melamine. Under the food/feed contamination category, the report tells us there is "*literature evidence for previous nephrotoxicity outbreak in pets in Asia in 2004*" and "*Literature data shows widespread contamination of fish and meat meal with melamine in Italy in the period 1979-1987.*" (19)

China has had the opportunity to properly dispose of melamine-tainted products and properly control food related industries at risk of melamine tainting since 1979...and they obviously haven't. The assumption that this new melamine find (76 tons) is left over from 2008 is giving far more credit to China than is due.

Management of a Deadly Recall

During the 2007 Pet Food Recall a public relations firm was hired to 'handle' the bad press pet food was taking. During the 'handling,' countless pets continued to die.

Hired to "*manage*" the deadliest pet food recall in history, Gene Grabowski, chair of crisis and litigation practice at Levick Strategic Communications, recently spoke to Newsweek magazine regarding the handling of Toyota's latest recall. Regarding the 2007 pet food recall, Mr. Grabowski told Newsweek his firm "*got vets to go on pet blogs and post information that 98% of pet food was safe*". He stated his firm knew the two most credible sources of information for pet owners were "*other pet owners and veterinarians*". So, Levick Strategic Communications 'got veterinarians' to calm pet owners nerves; "*mitigated consumer anxiety*". (20)

Hmmm...98% of pet food was safe as Mr. Grabowski's firm told veterinarians to tell pet owners? Let's look at the list of recalled pet foods in 2007...

Cat Food Recalls
Americas Choice, Preferred Pet
Authority
Best Choice
Blue Buffalo Co (RICE GLUTEN)
Cats Choice
Co-Op Gold
Companion
Compliments
Demolulas Market Basket
Demoulas/Market Basket
Despar
Diamond Pet Food (RICE GLUTEN)
Doctors Foster & Smith
Doctors Foster & Smith (RICE GLUTEN)

Eight In One Inc (Salmonella)
Eukanuba Cat Cuts and Flaked
Eukanuba Morsels in Gravy
Evolve
Evolve
Fame
Feline Classic
Feline Cuisine
Fine Feline Cat
Food Lion
Foodtown
Giant Companion
Giant Eagle
Hannaford
Harmony Farms (RICE GLUTEN)
Hartz Mountain Corp (Salmonella)
Health Diet Cat Food
Hill Country Fare
Hill's Prescription Diet
Hy Vee
Hy-Vee
Iams Cat Slices and Flakes
Iams Select Bites
J.E. Mondou
La Griffe
Laura Lynn
Li'l Red
Lick Your Chops
Lick Your Chops (RICE GLUTEN)
Loving Meals
Master Choice
Medi-Cal
Meijer's Main Choice
Natural Balance (RICE GLUTEN)
Natural Ultramix
Nu Pet
Nutriplan
Nutro
Nutro Max Cat Gourmet Classics

Nutro Max Gourmet Classics
Nutro Natural Choice
Nutro Products
Paws
Performatrin Ultra
Pet Pride
Pet Pride / Good n Meaty
Pounce
Presidents Choice
Price Chopper
Priority Canada
Priority US
Publix
Roche Brothers
Roundy's
Royal Canin (RICE GLUTEN)
Royal Canin Veterinary Diet (RICE GLUTEN)
Save-A-Lot Special Blend
Schnucks
Science Diet Feline Cuts Adult
Science Diet Feline Cuts Kitten
Science Diet Feline Cuts Mature Adult 7+
Science Diet Feline Savory Cuts Can
Sophistacat
Special Kitty Canada
Special Kitty US
Springfield Prize
Sprout
Stop & Shop Companion
Stuzzy Gold
Triumph
Wegmans
Weis Total Pet
Western Family Canada
Western Family US
White Rose
Winn Dixie
Your Pet

Dog Food Recalls
ALPO
Americas Choice, Preferred Pet
Authority
Award
Berkley & Jenson (Salmonella)
Best Choice
Big Bet
Big Red
Bloom
Blue Buffalo (RICE GLUTEN)
Bruiser
Cadillac
Canine Caviar Pet Foods (RICE GLUTEN)
Champion Breed Lg Biscuit
Champion Breed Peanut Butter Biscuits
Co-Op Gold
Companion
Companion's Best Multi-Flavor Biscuit
Compliments
Costco/Kirkland Signature (RICE GLUTEN)
Demoulas Market Basket
Diamond Pet Food
Diamond Pet Food (RICE GLUTEN)
Doctors Foster & Smith
Doctors Foster & Smith (RICE GLUTEN)
Dollar General
Eight In One Inc (Salmonella)
Eukanuba Can Dog Chunks in Gravy
Eukanuba Pouch Dog Bites in Gravy
Food Lion
Giant Companion
Gravy Train
Grreat Choice
Hannaford
Happy Tails
Harmony Farms (RICE GLUTEN)
Harmony Farms Treats (RICE GLUTEN)

Health Diet Gourmet Cuisine
Hill Country Fare
Hy Vee
Hy-Vee
Iams Can Chunky Formula
Iams Can Small Bites Formula
Iams Dog Select Bites
Jerky Treats Beef Flavored Dog Snacks
La Griffe
Laura Lynn
Loving Meals
Mars Petcare US Inc (Salmonella)
Master Choice
Meijer's Main Choice
Mighty Dog
Mixables
Mulligan Stew Pet Food (RICE GLUTEN)
Natural Balance (RICE GLUTEN)
Natural Life
Natural Way
Nu Pet
Nutriplan
Nutro
Nutro - Ultra
Nutro Max
Nutro Natural Choice
Nuture
Ol' Roy
Ol' Roy 4-Flavor Lg Biscuits
Ol' Roy Canada
Ol' Roy Peanut Butter Biscuits
Ol' Roy Puppy
Ol'Roy (Salmonella)
Ol'Roy US
Ol'Roy US (Salmonella)
Paws
Perfect Pals Large Biscuits
Performatrin Ultra
Pet Essentials

Pet Life
Pet Pride / Good n Meaty
Petrapport Inc. (Salmonella)
Presidents Choice
Price Chopper
Priority Canada
Priority US
Publix
Roche Brothers
Royal Canin (RICE GLUTEN)
Royal Canin Veterinary Diet (RICE GLUTEN)
Save-A-Lot Choice Morsels
Schnuck's
Schnucks
Shep
Shep Dog
Shop Rite
SmartPak (RICE GLUTEN)
Springfield Prize
Sprout
Stater Brothers
Stater Brothers Large Biscuits
Stop & Shop Companion
T.W. Enterpriese (Salmonella)
Tops Companion
Triumph
Truly
Weis Total Pet
Western Family Canada
Western Family US
White Rose
Winn Dixie
Your Pet

Hard to believe the previous list is only 2% of all pet foods, isn't it? Considering Colgate Palmolive, maker of Science Diet, Proctor & Gamble, maker of Iams, Eukanuba and Mars Petcare maker of Royal Canin, Nutro are three of the top five pet food producers in retail sales in the world (Mars Petcare being the leader at $11.8 billion in sales in 2007) are included in the

'2% list', I simply can't understand the math that was used to arrive at the quoted "*98% of all pet food was safe*". (21)

Although there were reports of over 18,000 pets that became ill and or died due to melamine-poisoned vegetable proteins in 2007, I'd like for you to read words from one pet owner whose four legged best friend died due to the '2% of not safe pet food'…(this pet owner recently wrote Judge Maughmer regarding the sentencing of ChemNutra executives)…

"Dear Judge Maughmer,

I understand that you are getting ready to sentence ChemNutra. As you are contemplating the sentence, I hope you consider all of the emotional pain this company has caused. I spent agonizing months attempting to pull my little dog back from the brink that was caused by this company. In the final days, Merlin and I sat next to each other, he in a tank attached to oxygen and I on the bedroom floor next to him so that he wouldn't feel alone. I'm disabled and it was not easy, but I was determined that Merlin knew he hadn't done anything to warrant his isolation. In the end, I held him in my arms while my veterinarian administered a lethal dosage that would finally separate me from my dear friend. It cost $6000 in vet bills, several friendships, and almost a marriage. I cried for months. Please make sure ChemNutra pays for this horrible crime."

Merlin

Now, imagine this heartbreaking story repeated 18,000 times (some estimates are 350,000 pets died).

The criminals that imported the melamine-tainted vegetable proteins responsible for the death of at least 18,000 beloved pets – Steven and Sally Miller of ChemNutra - were fined merely $25,000, a slap on the hand for pet deaths. It is reported that today they have a new import business.

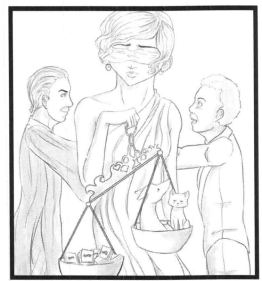

**THOUSANDS DEAD, CHEM NUTRA SENTENCED
PROBATION & FINE OF $25,000**

While the Millers begin their new business life, thousands of pet owners still wait for the settlement of the lawsuit won against Menu Foods. Four years later, no disbursement of settlement money has been provided to pet owners.

U.S. or China

US pet owners have believed that Chinese companies are solely to blame in the numerous cases of tainted pet foods over the last several years. Information provided to TruthaboutPetFood.com tells a slightly different story. It has been reported that one US pet food and pet treat distributor instructed a Chinese manufacturer to add melamine to dog treats.

I was one of those US pet owners. I believed the deaths and illnesses of thousands of US and Canadian dogs and cats were due to reckless Chinese manufacturers. The more Chinese recalls that occurred (toothpaste, tires, drywall), the more it seemed to me that China had no quality control of any type of product manufacturing.

I received an email from a Chinese pet treat manufacturer, the sole supplier of dog and cat treats for a US company most pet owners would be familiar with. The US company sells many different types of dog and cat treats and several different varieties of dog and cat foods. I corresponded several times with this representative of the Chinese manufacturer. He answered every one of my questions directly and openly. Knowing more information than I can report because of lawsuit risks from the US pet treat and pet food company, I believe the Chinese manufacturer. Below is a direct quote from his emails. The US company name and company owner has been XXX-ed out due to legal threats. You decide who you believe.

"Subject: XXX is unsafe and not as advertised

Question/Comment: My family has been producing the XXX brand of dog treats in China for the past 4 years and recently they terminated our contract after we were told to report all irradiated pet food products to the Chinese government. This was an unfair blow to our business after following exact directions by the owner and founder Mr. XXXX, to 1. Irradiate the chicken and product as needed, 2. for financial reasons, use only 65% chicken and the remainder to be non-fowl filler ... including melamine, peanuts, bone fragment powder, etc ... and 3. even though they advertised to use vitamins and herbs for stronger bones, etc., we never were allowed to include these because the cost would be too much.

XXX recently acquired 80% of the company for almost $20mm USD in December of 2008, and knew the product produced was in fact not as advertised. XXX was the lead investor for XXX and he was fully aware of the false advertising and potentially dangerous products being used. As early as January they were informed of the full ingredients used and in fact informed our factory to continue shipping up until this past week when our contract was wrongly terminated.

We followed our directions from Mr. XXX and now we are paying the price so he can retain his face and destroy the reputation of our family. XXX is and has been a false product from the beginning. Please feel free to communicate with XXX and XXX further as we are being threatened to keep quiet by legal means.

Thank you,
XXX"

I urged the Chinese company to report this to the USDA and to the FDA. They agreed and shared with me that they will report it immediately. I have reported the US company to the FDA as well, forwarding all of the correspondence between myself and the Chinese company to the FDA.

The US company that sells this dog and cat treat (as well as other treats and a line of foods) emphasizes the word 'natural' in their advertising. If it is true what the Chinese manufacturer reports, the dog and cat treats sold as 'natural' all over the US should be relabeled as 'deadly'. The ingredient list is apparently completely false, and the treat is very likely permanently damaging the kidneys of countless dogs and cats as you are reading this.

Days following publishing this story on TruthaboutPetFood.com, I received a phone call from the President of a U.S. pet food/treat manufacturer. His call to me was to profess his company's innocence (despite no mention of any manufacturer in the article - was I talking about him?...why did he think I was?). During the same time frame, a rather harsh comment - in opposition to the article - was posted on Truthabout-PetFood.com. A quick IP address search of the post (location and owner of the computer that posted the negative comment) turned out to be the Investment firm heavily invested in the same U.S. pet food/treat manufacturer professing their innocence.

Guilty? Because I was never provided with evidence (follow up communication with Chinese manufacturer stated he and his family were threatened by the U.S. company), we will never know for certain.

Pet Food Personal Experience - Cody

Cody (right) & Cooper (left)

    Cody was my first dog. My husband and I argued for years about getting a dog, but I just didn't want one. Finally after 5 years of his moaning and groaning, I gave in. My world was changed forever. Cody, a white and gold Shih Tzu, was just shy of 6 weeks when we brought him home. He slept the entire 45 minute car ride in the crook of my neck and I never looked back. He became the heart and soul of our family and was cherished beyond words.

    In October of 2006, when Cody was just a year and 1/2 old, he became sick. His kidneys began to fail. We drove him 2 hours to the nearest teaching hospital where he spent a week in the ICU. No one could figure out what was causing this young pup's kidneys to fail. Every test came back negative for disease, but his kidneys were out right failing. After a week, they decided to let us take him home and hope for a miracle. They hoped he would get better on his own, being at home, surrounded by love and being given sub q fluids. It was our only hope. For weeks he slept all day, he was weak, he didn't want to eat and the sparkle in his eyes was gone. But we loved him and cared for him with every bone in our bodies and before we knew it, he was better.

The doctors couldn't quite explain it. His kidney levels were still that of a very sick dog, but he was happy again, full of life and he wasn't going to give up. He had chronic kidney failure. Meaning his kidneys were failing, but he was living with it. A few months later, our other Shih Tzu, Cooper, also just one year old, became ill. He is of no relation to Cody, but they were best friends and brothers at heart. Cooper never got as sick as Cody did, but his kidney levels were rising just as Cody's had and at this point stories of the recalls were hitting the news. At that point we knew. The vets knew. It was the food we were feeding our babies, the food we expected to provide them with a long, healthy life, that was slowly poisoning them from the inside out.

We switched our boys from Nutro Ultra and Nutro Naturals to Chicken Soup for the Puppy Lover's Soul. I was only able to purchase it at a specialty shop and they seemed to love it. I was confident this food would not harm my boys. Little did I know, this too would be recalled within a few weeks. So my boys were fed not one, not two, but 3 different brands of recalled food. Talk about a wake up call.

I took both Cody and Cooper off of dog food immediately. Fool me once, shame on you, fool me twice, shame on me. And I felt so guilty. Why hadn't I taken them off of dog food sooner? I began preparing their meals for them at home. Every day, cooking a new meal. They thrived, but the damage was irreversible.

Cody lived until May 12, 2010 when his kidneys finally had enough. This was the most horrible day of our lives! Our baby boy was gone. All because he trusted us to feed him something healthy. All because I blindly trusted the pet food companies to provide sustenance to my boys. Cody paid the ultimate price.

Cooper is left without a brother, without a playmate. We are left with a hole in our hearts and an immeasurable rage. Cooper is still living and thriving on his home cooked diet. He lives with chronic kidney disease. Thankfully, he was not poisoned as much as Cody was. His kidneys are not failing, they are just damaged. At 5 years old, he is what keeps us going.

We all miss our Cody Bear more than words can explain. He is gone, he died at 5 years old all because of the food he ate. All because of the corruption in the pet food industry. Something must be done. People need to wake up and see the truth.

Rest in peace sweet Cody Bear. If love could have saved you, you would have lived forever.

Buyer Beware

Cody Bear 04/02/05 - 05/12/10
Christian Kay B.

How Horrible Can Pet Food Ingredients Get?

To start, you should understand that the pet food industry began by doing about the same thing that pet owners used to do…feed their dogs and cats leftovers from family meals. Corporations saw the opportunity with leftover ingredients from the manufacturing and processing of human food and commercial pet food was born. While leftovers from your family dinner don't sound too harmful for pets, leftovers from the commercial side can be quite different.

Interestingly enough, back in the 1960's the pet food industry initiated a nationwide campaign warning pet owners of the 'dangers' of feeding your dog or cat leftovers. Yet they themselves did and continue to do the very same on a commercial level.

It must be stated before the graphic descriptions begin, that the disgusting items discussed below are, in fact, illegal to be processed into any food including dog and cat food. Despite (or perhaps in spite of) the Federal Food, Drug, and Cosmetic Act which clearly states no food, human food or animal food, can contain any part of a diseased or euthanized animal, an FDA (Federal Food and Drug Administration) compliance policy allows any diseased animal and any euthanized animal to become dog and cat food ingredients.

Although the topic has rarely been discussed in main stream media, a few brave journalists (and certainly brave editors) have discussed the 'The Dark Side of Recycling' which is the title of Keith Woods' article published in 1990. His original story was published by the San Francisco Chronicle. However, this version was *"watered down."* Earth Island Journal published his complete story in the fall of 1990.

The first couple of paragraphs from *"The Dark Side of Recycling"*.....

"A RENDERING PLANT SOMEWHERE IN SOUTHERN CALIFORNIA -- The rendering plant floor is piled high with "raw product". Thousands of dead dogs and cats; heads and hooves from cattle, sheep, pigs and horses; whole skunks; rats and raccoons -- all waiting to be processed. In the 90 degree heat, the

piles of dead animals seem to have a life of their own as millions of maggots swarm over the carcasses.

Two bandanna-masked men begin operating Bobcat mini-dozers, loading the "raw" into a ten-foot deep stainless steel pit. They are undocumented workers from Mexico doing a dirty job. A giant auger-grinder at the bottom of the pit begins to turn. Popping bones and squeezing flesh are sounds from a nightmare you will never forget." (22)

In September, 1995 Baltimore City Paper Journalist Van Smith provided readers with another graphic description. This is the beginning of his story "What's Cookin'?".....

"Consider these items: Bozman, the Baltimore City Police Department quarter horse who died last summer in the line of duty. The grill grease and used frying oil from Camden Yards, the city's summer ethnic festivals, and nearly all Baltimore-area and Ocean City restaurants and hotels. A baby circus elephant who died while in Baltimore this summer. Millions of tons of waste meat and inedible animal parts from the region's supermarkets and slaughter-houses. Carcasses from the Baltimore Zoo. The thousands of dead dogs, cats, raccoons, possums, deer, foxes, snakes, and the rest that local animal shelters and road-kill patrols must dispose of each month.

"These are the raw materials of Baltimore's fat-and-protein econ-omy, which are processed into marketable products for high profit at the region's only rendering plant in Curtis Bay. In a gruesomely ironic twist, most inedible dead-animal parts, including dead pets, end up in feed used to fatten up future generations of their kind." (23)

In the spring of 1996, Earth Island Journal published 'Food not Fit for a Pet' by Wendell O. Belfield, DVM. The following is an excerpt from his story...

"For seven years, I was a veterinary meat inspector for the US Department of Agriculture and the State of California. I waded through blood, water, pus and fecal material, inhaled the fetid stench from the killing floor and listened to the death cries of slaughtered animals.

Prior to World War II, most slaughterhouses were all-inclusive; that is, live-stock was slaughtered and processed in one location. There was a section for smoking meats, a section for processing meats into sausages and a section for rendering.

After World War II, the meat industry became more specialized. A slaughterhouse dressed the carcasses, while a separate facility made the sausages. The rendering of slaughter waste also became a separate specialty -- no longer within the jurisdiction of federal meat inspectors and out of the public eye.

To prevent condemned meat from being rerouted and used for human consumption, government regulations require that meat is "denatured" before removal from the slaughterhouse and shipment to rendering facilities. In my time as a veterinary meat inspector, we denatured with carbolic acid (a potentially corrosive disinfectant) and/or creosote (used for wood-preservation or as a disinfectant). Both substances are highly toxic. According to federal meat inspection regulations, fuel oil, kerosene, crude carbolic acid and citronella (an insect repellent made from lemon grass) all are approved denaturing materials.

Condemned livestock carcasses treated with these chemicals can become meat and bone meal for the pet food industry. Because rendering facilities are not government controlled, any animal carcasses can be rendered -- even dogs and cats. As Eileen Layne of the CVMA told the Chronicle, "When you read pet food labels, and it says 'meat and bone meal,' that's what it is: cooked and converted animals, including some dogs and cats." (24)

Pet food ingredients that could come from the rendering examples above are:
> **Animal Fat**
> **Meat and Bone Meal**
> **Meat Meal**
> **Animal Digest**

What is Rendering?

As you've probably figured out, rendering is the process of taking the nastiest of the nasty and turning it into something sellable. The industry calls itself 'the original recyclers'.

From a 2004 Report prepared for Congress titled *"Animal Rendering: Economics and Policy"*...

"Renderers convert dead animals and animal byproducts into ingredients for a wide range of industrial and consumer goods, such as animal feed, soaps, candles, pharmaceuticals, and personal care products. U.S. regulatory actions to bolster safeguards against bovine spongiform encephalopathy (BSE or mad cow disease) could portend significant changes in renderers' business practices, the value of their products and, consequently, the balance sheets of animal producers and processors. Also, if animal byproducts have fewer market outlets, questions arise about how to dispose of them safely. This report, which will not be updated, describes the industry and discusses several industry-related issues that have arisen in the 108th Congress."

"Renderers convert dead animals and animal parts that otherwise would require disposal into a variety of materials, including edible and inedible tallow and lard and proteins such as meat and bone meal (MBM). These materials in turn are exported or sold to domestic manufacturers of a wide range of industrial and consumer goods such as livestock feed and pet food, soaps, pharmaceuticals, lubricants, plastics, personal care products, and even crayons."

(bold added)
"Renderers annually convert 47 billion pounds or more of raw animal materials into approximately 18 billion pounds of products. Sources for these materials include *meat slaughtering and processing plants (the primary one);* **dead animals from farms, ranches, feedlots, marketing barns, animal shelters**, *and other facilities; and fats, grease, and other food waste from restaurants and stores."*

Yes...a report prepared for the 108th Congress of the United States told elected officials that dead animals from animal shelters are cooked (rendered) and converted into pet food and crayons. Despite this being a clear violation of Federal law, not one Representative of Congress did a thing about it.

(Some) Pet food is dumping ground for 'Specified Risk Materials'

While imported ingredients remain high on the awareness of pet owners across the US and Canada, there is something right here in the US that few are aware of which poses a similar threat to our pets. The FDA terms the ingredients SRM's – specified risk materials. SRM's were once a common pet food ingredient that is little more than waste from the human meat industry. The name alone – Specified Risk Materials – explains the concern.

A common concern discussed by those in the know about pet food is known as the 4-D ingredients. The 4-D's are dead, diseased, drugged, and downed meat producing animals. These 4-D animals are rejected for use in human food for apparent reasons. Common sense would cause one to assume the animals are destroyed, but that is not the case. 4-D animals are processed for use in pet food and are one part of the FDA's Specified Risk Materials.

Another concern of SRM's comes from a more modern day risk of mad cow disease – BSE - Bovine Spongiform Encephalopathy. The FDA's definition of BSE is *"Bovine spongiform encephalopathy (BSE) is a chronic, degenerative disorder affecting the central nervous system of cattle."* (25)

To give the FDA credit, it has stepped up control a great deal in recent years and does not allow SRM's to be introduced into the human food chain by prohibiting any possible SRM's into the feed of cattle, sheep, or pigs – ruminant animals. Recent FDA regulations no longer allow SRM's to be added to pet food as well. However, many believe SRM's – despite new regulations prohibiting their use in pet food – mad cow disease specified risk materials still ultimately end up in pet food.

To provide you with some startling numbers explaining just how much Specified Risk Material is processed, I will quote a letter from Garth Merrick (of Merrick Pet Food) to the FDA…*"Federal Measures To Mitigate BSE Risks: Considerations for Further Action"*….

"SRM's in cattle under 30 months of age have been estimated to be 20 pounds per head. In Texas there are four packing houses processing approximately 100,000 head per week times 20 pounds equals 2,000,000 times 52 weeks equals 104,000,000 of product that no one has discussed what to do with. Also, in Texas, there are approximately 18,000 head of cows over 30 months of age slaughtered weekly at four packing plants which have approximately 60 pounds per head of SRM material equals 1,080,000 per week equals 56,160,000 pounds per year. Our company services mostly Texas and parts of New Mexico, Oklahoma and Kansas. Last year we processed

255,000 head of dead stock not counting calves with an average weight of 600 pounds per carcass. The total weight comes to 153,000.000 pounds that makes its way into feed ingredients."

The 4-D material discussed above – from one company – processed 153 million pounds of dead cattle in one year. I repeat – 153 million pounds of processed dead cattle in one year from one company! There is no testing to determine the reason the animal died. Causes could run from old age to disease. We just don't know. The current FDA and AAFCO regulations allow dead (4-D) animals to be processed into pet food. They are not allowed to be processed into the human food chain either directly or indirectly (through use in cattle or pig feed).

Mr. Merrick's letter to the FDA does bring up the valid point of what should the processors of meat do with these millions and millions of pounds of SRM's? I don't have an answer to that question. But I can tell you that I don't want SRM's in my pet's food bowl. It should not be pet food's responsibility to find a selling point for SRM's.

Pet Food Protein

Pet food regulations require an adult cat food to provide a minimum of 26% protein and an adult dog food to provide a minimum of 18% protein; however, the regulations aren't too picky about the source of and/or the quality of protein used to meet the percentage requirements. Everything from choice cuts of meat to grains to diseased, rendered animals are used as protein in pet foods.

A northwest Arkansas newspaper article reporting on the poultry industry recently provided the perfect introduction to the discussion of quality of pet food protein; "*Poultry companies have found a market for everything but the cluck…*"

Providing industries the ability to sell 'everything but the cluck', the FDA allows animal farmers a sales outlet for the un-sellable; sick, diseased, and euthanized animals are commonly sold to pet food manufacturers. Health conscious individuals (and plain old sane people) would expect diseased, condemned livestock to be destroyed. Unfortunately, such is not the case. Diseased poultry and other diseased animals are commonly processed into pet food.

In the most recent FDA Food Safety Inspection Services (FSIS) Directive (dated 4/30/09), the FDA instructs food inspectors to condemn 'suspect' poultry that shows signs of disease. *"Signs of disease that inspection program personnel may observe on ante-mortem inspection include swelling about the head and eyes, edema of the wattles, gasping and sneezing, off-colored feces, diarrhea, skin lesions, lameness, torticollosis (e.g., wry neck), and bone or joint enlargement."* (26)

Similar to all other condemned diseased livestock, condemned poultry and 'dead on arrival poultry' must be disposed of according to regulations. As you read the FSIS regulation of 'Handling and Disposal of Condemned Other Inedible Products at Official Establishments', keep in mind these materials are 'disposed of' in many dog foods, cat foods, and pet treats.

Sec. 381.95 Disposal of condemned poultry products.
"All condemned carcasses, or condemned parts of carcasses… shall be disposed of by one of the following methods…
(a) Steam treatment or thorough cooking in a kettle or vat, for a sufficient time to effectively destroy the product for human food pur-poses…
(b) Incineration or complete destruction by burning.
(c) Chemical denaturing, which shall be accomplished by the lib-eral application to all carcasses and parts thereof, of:
(1) Crude carbolic acid,
(2) Kerosene, fuel oil, or used crankcase oil, or…"

Condemned poultry is cooked via rendering *"to effectively destroy the product for human food purposes"*, incinerated and completely destroyed (which provides the farmer with no possible revenue and which thusly is unlikely to occur) or treated with harsh denaturing chemicals such as kerosene or oil. Option (a) or (c) poultry, rendering and harsh chemical denaturing, become sellable products to pet food manufacturers including the denaturing agents such as kerosene or used crankcase oil. Rendered and chemical denatured condemned poultry and livestock can become the common pet food ingredients 'by-product' (such as chicken by-product or poultry by-product), 'by-product meal' (similar examples of specific animal sources), 'meat and bone meal', 'meat meal' (not to be confused with pet food ingredient chicken meal or turkey meal – 'meat meal' is generic and can be any type of animal), and 'animal digest'. It should also be noted that the fat that rises to the top of the vat in the rendering of these condemned livestock can become the common pet food ingredient 'animal fat'.

The quality of these protein sources is highly questionable, at best. However, despite the obvious risk from utilizing these type of ingredients in pet foods, *"the Center for Veterinary Medicine (CVM) is aware of no instances of disease or other hazard occurring…"* from their use; thus the FDA's approval for these types of protein sources in pet foods.

Another common source of protein utilized by many pet food manufacturers is vegetable proteins. Grains such as corn, wheat, and soy are often used as an economical source of protein in dog foods and cat foods alike. As well, vegetable protein concentrates such as corn gluten or rice protein are inexpensively added to pet food formulas to boost protein percentages in lieu of quality meat proteins.

The optimal source of protein in cat foods and dog foods is quality meat proteins, the same quality of meat you would purchase for any other member of your family. While many pet foods primarily use USDA quality meats, these manufacturers are not allowed to provide you this information on the pet food label. The regulations state there can be no reference to grade or quality.

Protein options in pet foods can range from pet grade meats (not suitable or approved for human consumption), vegetable protein sources, or human grade meats. In order to know what type of protein is provided in your pet's food, start by reading the ingredient label. Protein sources are typically listed within the first five to ten ingredients. If your pet's food lists several (three or more) meat proteins such as 'chicken', 'turkey', 'chicken meal', 'salmon', 'salmon meal' (and similar), you can safely assume the majority of protein percentage is derived from meat. If your pet's food label lists several vegetable protein sources such as 'corn', 'soy', 'corn gluten' (and similar), you can safely assume a significant percentage of protein comes from vegetable sources. And finally, if your pet's food label lists one or more by-product, meat and bone meal, meat meal, and/or animal digest, you can safely assume a significant percentage of protein comes from pet grade meats.

But how can you determine if your pet's food uses a human grade or quality of meat? Although the above seems to be a fairly clear method to determine the protein sources of your pet's food, there is actually very little that is 'clear' when it comes to pet food. According to pet food regulations, there is NO definition of human grade or human quality meat. Furthermore, because pet food regulations do not allow pet food labels to inform petsumers of the quality or grade of meat ingredients (added to the dilemma of no official definition), pet owners must call or email the specific manufacturer to ask what quality or grade of meat is used in the pet food, relying on the manufacturer's representative to provide an honest, informed answer.

My own experiences from asking this question hundreds of times ('Is the grade of meat used in your pet food a human grade meat or pet grade meat?'), has provided a variety of responses varying from honest to downright lies. Without virtually being at the pet food manufacturer during the processing of every batch of food, without virtually inspecting the health condition of every meat producing animal prior to processing the pet food, without knowing if the poultry feed or cattle feed was not laced with drugs before processing the animal for food, and on and on, pet owners are left with taking the word of the manufacturer. With the recalls of recent years, taking the word of any pet food manufacturer is challenging.

One possible assurance of the quality of meat protein ingredients is APHIS EU certification. Animal Plant Health Inspection Services (APHIS) is a division of the USDA. Some pet food manufacturers have certified their manufacturing facilities APHIS EU (European Union). When a pet food is manufactured in the United States and exported to Europe for sale, the manufacturing plant must have APHIS EU certification (export requirements of pet foods to Europe are far more stringent than for US made and US sold pet foods). This certification requires that all meat ingredients are USDA human grade, the pet food manufacturing plant is inspected and approved by the USDA, and ingredient suppliers are inspected and approved by the USDA. Pet food manufacturers that sell dog food and cat food brands in Europe, that do NOT meet APHIS EU certification (which are many), have their own manufacturing facilities in Europe (versus exporting).

There are many pet food manufacturing facilities that are APHIS EU certified that do not export their products to Europe. It could be these manufacturers have future plans to export to European pet owners, or it could be these manufacturers wish to provide pet owners with a bit of assurance of quality. Regardless, to date, APHIS EU certification of a pet food manufacturing plant is the best method we have to assure the quality or grade of meat protein ingredients in lieu of grazing our own meat producing animals, growing all the necessary ingredients, and producing our own pet foods. Call your pet food manufacturer and ask if their facility is APHIS EU certified. My experience from asking this question is almost humorous. Eighty percent (plus) of pet food customer service representatives did not understand what I was asking about, a clue that the manufacturer is not certified.

Pet food manufacturers that are not APHIS EU certified does not guarantee they are using a lower quality pet grade meat. However, without the certification, pet owners are left to taking their word on quality.

There are several pet food ingredients that, if you knew exactly what they were, would probably send you running. It's sort of like what people say about bologna, 'if you knew what went into it...' – times ten. The bigger problem is that only a handful of individuals (rendering industry employees) really know what goes into popular pet food ingredients such as by-product meal, meat and bone meal, beef and bone meal, animal fat, and animal digest..... and they're not talking.

Risk of Pentobarbital

The FDA website provides a report titled 'Report on the risk from pentobarbital in dog food'. (27). Briefly, in the late 1990's the FDA, under pressure from practicing veterinarians, tested dog foods (no cat foods were tested) to determine if they contained pentobarbital, the drug used to euthanize animals. Their findings were that many popular dog foods do indeed contain pentobarbital; thus these popular pet foods contain some type of euthanized animal. The FDA determined that the common pet food ingredients 'Meat and Bone Meal', 'Beef and Bone Meal', 'Animal Fat', and 'Animal Digest' appeared to be the link to the presence of pentobarbital.

FDA testing found the drug in Nutro, Ol' Roy, Ken-L-Ration, Kibbles 'n Bits, Purina Pro Plan dog food among others. (28)

You'd think that after the FDA report was published in 2002, every pet food manufacturer that used these ingredients would change their formulations utilizing a seemingly safer ingredient or at the very least provide pet owners with certified laboratory tests on their websites proving that their pentobarbital-suspect ingredients are clean of the lethal drug. You'd think that, but that's not the case.

Any sane person would also assume that all of the pet foods that tested positive for pentobarbital (thus certain to contain a euthanized animal) would have been immediately recalled. That didn't happen either.

Instead, many pet food manufacturers, many of the top selling brands in the U.S., continue to use meat and bone meal, beef and bone meal, animal fat, and/or animal digest in their pet foods and treats choosing to ignore the FDA research and as well choosing not to provide their customers with any ingredient safety information.

Flavored Words

One popular dog food manufacturer has decided to add pleasant descriptive language on its ingredient list following one of the FDA recognized pentobarbital suspect ingredient animal digest.

On the label of one variety of dog food, the ingredient list states *"animal digest (source of chicken flavor)"*. On another variety of dog food, the ingredient list states *"animal digest (source of grilled flavor)"*. It's difficult to imagine that a diseased euthanized animal, ground up into tiny pieces, thrown into a large vat and cooked with other euthanized diseased animals could be a source of any flavor, never the less to provide multiple flavors like 'chicken' and 'grilled flavor'.

We have to assume that since large corporations don't do anything without substantial consumer research, they learned that consumers felt the words 'animal digest' alone sounded a bit offensive. We can guess that consumer research told them *"animal digest (source of chicken flavor)"* and *"animal digest (source of grilled flavor)"* sounded much more appealing. We also have to assume that this pet food company feels that as long as these descriptive terms sell dog food, who cares if it's stretching the truth and who cares if this ingredient might contain a euthanized animal.

So if you notice on your pet food or pet treat label 'chicken flavor' or 'grilled flavor', you might want to check the ingredient list to see if it contains anything on the FDA list of pentobarbital suspect ingredients. The 'mystery meat' flavoring might not be what you want to feed your dog or cat.

Pet Food and Rendering Plants

The following is a personal account of a Rendering Facility, by Jerry E.

First let me introduce myself. I am a retired Certified Pest Control Operator. I was certified in three states. I have an associate degree in entomology, food grade warehouse management, and several courses in sanitation. I serviced and advised large national meatpacking plants, other food manufacturing plants, feed mills, and pet food plants. I worked closely with the USDA inspectors and quality control departments of several plants including the pet food plants. The largest pet food plant manufactured pet food for 65 different companies and took up a majority of my time the last few years of my business.

My first experience with rendering plants were those that were in the tail end of the meatpacking plants. They were good clean rendering plants, if there is such a thing. The only thing they rendered was the waste from the cattle they processed. There was never any outside product brought in. The rendering plant was separated from the main plant by a concrete wall. The components to be rendered were augured in from the main plant and ground into small pieces, then put in a cooker and heated at 280 degrees for approximately an hour, usually a little more. The cooking eliminated the moisture, and then the product was run through a screening process that separated the product into bone

60

meal, protein meal and larger bone fragments and fat. Very little of this product went to pet food manufactures.

My first experience with an independent rendering plant that rendered product for pet food was totally shocking. I suppose I was partially prepared for it by the meatpacking plants, but this was still shocking. At any rate, the local plant called me because they were expecting a corporate representative to come in the following month, and they had a horrendous rat problem. They wanted to show corporate that they had the problem under control. I am going to try to remember this plant in detail to give you an idea of what goes into our pet foods. That is not to say that they are all this way, but this is a general example that I ran into more often than I would have expected.

The plant was out in the middle of an open field and, except for a 15 foot parameter around the building, the weeds were waist to neck high. I entered the plant on a dirt drive that went up to a concrete parking slab in the front of the building; in front of the office door and a large overhead door. The dirt drive went around one side of the building to the back where there was a concrete dump area with an overhead door going into the building. The concrete slab was sloped away from the building with a curb on both sides so that they could wash down the area. This is where the dead animals, parts and pieces of animals and other things to be rendered or processed were dumped. Between the dirt drive area and the building was junk parts and equipment piled up that obviously housed a large colony of rats as you could see their trails in and out of the junk piles. The other dumping ground for machine parts, etc. out back was also full of rats. The concrete pad in the back where the trucks dumped their loads had rat holes lining the curb that ran along the sides.

As you might imagine, this area was loaded with flies; the piles of products were alive with maggots. It made it look like the whole pile of product was alive and moving. After the loads were dumped they were picked up by a bobcat (a miniature loader with a scoop on the front) and hauled inside the plant to the rendering pit. The plant had three undocumented workers doing the labor, including running the bobcat. The pit was a concrete hole with sloped sides that was about 8 to 10 feet deep and it had four sides that were about 7 feet long. There was a small seam 1 inch wide about 4 feet down that ran all the way around the pit. This seam, as the ones in the corners, had several rat holes in them, so rats were living in the rendering pit.

At the bottom of the pit was an auger grinder that ground the product and augured it out to a bin to be cooked. The cooker was in the back corner of the plant that took up about one third of the building. After it was cooked, it was pressed to eliminate the remaining moisture. Then it was separated it into different products and shipped off to one of their other plants to be further processed and packaged. I asked where the finish products were sent to; they said it was shipped to several different pet food plants. It seems the corporation had several rendering plants and contracts with numerous pet food plants. Not only were dead animals that died who knows how being rendered, but also live rats, a lot of rat droppings plus all the dirt and concrete fragments that were removed from the rat holes in the pit and piles of maggots. But 'that was ok' because it was just going for pet food. What they were concerned about was the constant maintenance that the rats were causing by digging holes in the concrete and chewing through hoses and electric lines.

Maintenance expenses were getting too high and something had to be done. That is why they called me. It took a couple of months, and several buckets of dead rats, but I did take care of their rat problem. In the meantime I found out where a lot of the dead animals and other scraps and pieces came from. There were dead cows, pigs, horses, chickens, various road kill, packaged meat from local supermarkets and waste from restaurants and fast food places. The most sickening thing that I saw was trucks that came from chicken farms; I call them chicken prisons that were supposedly full of dead chickens. When they dumped, 90% of the chickens were dead, however there was always a few that were still alive, if you could call that alive. They were mostly featherless and staggering around obviously sick and dying. They picked them up and threw them into the pit alive to be ground up with the rest of the dump. Most of the cattle from feed lots and farmers had plastic ear tags impregnated with Dursban or other insecticides that were placed there to ward off flies. These tags were not removed, they were ground up with the cattle and the plastic and Styrofoam containers that spoiled and rotten meat from the supermarkets came in. When I asked about the ear tags and the plastic and Styrofoam they said that they could not afford to pay someone to remove them or unpackage the spoiled meats from the supermarkets. "Besides, they would be eliminated from the end product through the rendering process."

The cattle from the feed lots were full of antibiotics and hormones; they are given these antibiotics and hormones in the feed that they ate. They are added at the feed mill in the feed lots. Feed lots keep records of such additives for the government inspectors that never show up, or if they do it would only be about once a year. If for some reason the cattle contract some illness in spite of the added antibiotics, they receive more antibiotics from the veterinarians that work for the feed lot. If the cattle die even after all of that, they go to the rendering plant. And guess what! The rendering plant operators don't care why they died of or what kind of drugs were pumped into them.

After all, it is just going into pet food, and some of it will be sold to feed mills and go into cattle feed or other feed. People won't be eating it." Fact of the mater is that people do end up eating it too. Poorer people that are barely getting by will buy canned dog food to eat because it is cheap. That bit of information came from the quality control department of a nationally known pet food manufacture that insisted that their canned product be fit for human consumption. Of course theirs was not a cheaper brand.

The point of this is that when you see meat byproducts listed on the label of your pet food, this could be what you could be feeding your pet. So when you see this on the label I would encourage you to think twice about purchasing the product."

50 States and Congress

From Alabama to Wyoming, every U.S. state allows illegal pet foods and treats to be sold to unknowing consumers. Each and every State Department of Agriculture could step in and enforce federal laws with pet food, but they don't. No one does.

Federal food safety laws are very specific. No food for humans or animals can contain a diseased animal or an animal that has died other than by slaughter. Thank goodness for these laws. No one would want to eat lasagna made with ground meat from a sick animal or a hamburger from an animal that has been euthanized (side order of lethal drug please). It would be unhealthy and certainly dangerous.

But...every U.S. state allows diseased animals and euthanized animals to be ground up and cooked into pet foods and treats. Don't our pets deserve to be protected from dangerous and unhealthy ground meat from sick animals and ground meat from animals that have been euthanized? Fifty State Department of Agriculture offices don't think so.

Each state is different. Some are stricter than others. As an example, Florida Department of Agriculture has the reputation of being tough; yet the agent in charge of pet food told me, "*You are right. They (pet food ingredients that would contain a diseased animal or a euthanized animal) are prohibited by law*", and then he added "*But, we're going to follow FDA advice*".

A Maryland independent pet store owner recently was visited by the Agriculture Inspector. This inspector pulled numerous products from the pet food store, several because of improper labeling, one because the company had not registered with the state. Despite being on top of their game in one perspective, Maryland still allows the sale of illegal pet foods and treats to be sold one aisle over from YOUR food in the grocery and major retail outlets.

Call, email, and or write your State Department of Agriculture. Tell them you feel federal laws should be enforced relating to pet food and pet treat safety. Tell them all pet foods that contain the ingredients meat and bone meal, beef and bone meal, animal fat and/or animal digest should be removed from store shelves immediately. Insist your state abide by federal law. Insist the pet foods and treats be removed from store shelves until the manufacturer proves they are not in violation of federal law. It is federal law. It should be enforced. Until it is, closely read the ingredients of your pet's food and treats. If the food or treat contains 'Meat and Bone Meal', 'Beef and Bone Meal', 'Animal Fat', or 'Animal Digest', the product is probably in violation of federal law. Do not feed it to your pet. Return any unused products to the store and tell the clerk this food/treat is in violation of federal law and request a full refund. Do not support pet food/treat manufacturers that disregard federal food safety laws. Do not purchase their products.

Euthanized Pets in Pet Food

While I understand it is challenging at best to believe the possibility that euthanized dogs and cats are rendered and become pet food and treat ingredients, the very real possibility remains. The following is further information taken from the FDA website.

In 2002, the FDA published a report titled 'Risk from Pentobarbital in Dog Food'. The report states "*During the 1990s, FDA's Center for Veterinary Medicine (CVM) received reports from veterinarians that pentobarbital, an anesthetizing agent used for dogs and other animals, seemed to be losing its effectiveness in dogs. Based on these reports, CVM officials decided to investigate a plausible theory that the dogs were exposed to pentobarbital through dog food, and that this exposure was making them less responsive to pentobarbital when it was used as a drug. In conjunction with this investigation, the Center wanted to determine if pet food contained rendered remains of dogs and cats."* (29)

I have my doubts that the CVM actually went to the extent of testing dog foods for pentobarbital simply because a few veterinarians complained that pentobarbital was losing its effectiveness. My theory is that CVM went to this extensive testing under pressure from the pet food industry, hoping to calm consumer panic that their pets might be consuming a pet food that contains a euthanized dog or cat. Fido having Fido for dinner was not a good publicity campaign for the booming pet food industry.

They succeeded in quieting major media by testing dog food and announcing that FDA/CVM testing found conclusive evidence that no dog or cat DNA was found in dog food. While this announcement was true, no dog or cat DNA was clinically discovered in dog food, it is far from the whole story.

The earlier (2002) studies of pentobarbital in dog food, *"did not address the central question of the source of the pentobarbital in dog food. It has been presumed that pentobarbital was present in these dog food samples because euthanized animals, such as dogs, cats, and horses, might be included with other animal byproducts used in preparing dog food. However, this presumption was difficult to test due to the limitations of existing analytical methods. Therefore, CVM scientists developed a polymerase chain reaction (PCR)-based approach to identify species-specific products that might be present in dog food."*

In this follow up test published in the FDA Veterinarian Newsletter January/February 2004, the FDA states the three possible sources of pentobarbital would be rendered euthanized dogs, cats, and or horses. Their testing was searching for dog DNA, cat DNA, or horse DNA. Their findings - No dog DNA was found, No cat DNA was found, and No horse DNA was found.

"The PCR results on the species of origin in the various dog food samples do not support a single point source of protein for the origin of the pentobarbital. While the results of this study narrow the search for the source of pentobarbital, it does not define the source (i.e., species) responsible for the contamination." (30)

The DNA testing performed by the CVM did find bovine (cow), swine, and/or sheep DNA in dog foods, but again, their testing found no species source of pentobarbital. Cows, pigs, and sheep are rarely euthanized with pentobarbital.

On one hand the FDA/CVM tells us that pentobarbital discovered in dog food would originate in euthanized dogs, cats, or horses. On the other hand, because the CVM testing found no dog, cat, or horse DNA in their testing, they made the profound statement that no pets are rendered into pet food based on inconclusive testing. To date, there is no clinical evidence to refute suspicions, hidden video, and personal accounts that euthanized dogs, cats, and possibly horses are rendered and become pet food ingredients. To date, neither pet owners nor the FDA know exactly how the lethal drug pentobarbital gets into pet food.

The one thing that is certain is that any dog food, cat food, or pet treat that contains pentobarbital would be a clear violation of the Federal Food, Drug, and Cosmetic Act. Strange that the FDA, the federal organization handed the responsibility of enforcing the Food, Drug, and Cosmetic Act, would not have immediately demanded all dog foods that tested positive for pentobarbital be recalled and deemed adulterated by federal law.

Again, ingredients at most risk to contain pentobarbital and thus a euthanized animal are meat and bone meal, beef and bone meal, animal fat, and animal digest.

U.S. Fish and Wildlife Services

Even though the FDA believes it is safe for our pets to consume Pentobarbital through pet food, the U.S. Fish and Wildlife Services (USFWS) disagrees. The following was taken from a USFWS report...

"*Secondary Pentobarbital Poisoning of Wildlife*"

"*Euthanasia by sodium pentobarbital injection is a humane way to end the life of a suffering animal, and is recommended for many species by the American Veterinary Medical Association (AVMA) Panel on Euthanasia.1 Ironically, this compassionate act can sometimes have the unintended consequence of causing the premature death of other animals. Each year a number of bald and golden eagles, other wildlife, and domestic dogs are intoxicated or killed after ingestion of pentobarbital residues in the tissue of exposed euthanized carcasses. Exposure of these carcasses is almost always the result of improper disposal."*

"Rendering is not an acceptable way to dispose of a pentobarbital-tainted carcass. The drug residues are not destroyed in the rendering process, so the tissues and by-products may contain poison and must not be used for animal feed."

Mycotoxins

Mycotoxins are deadly molds prone to grow on many common pet food ingredients. While many pet owners are familiar with aflatoxin contamination (causing pet food recalls in the past), a 2007 scientific report seems to suggest numerous mycotoxins, even at low levels over time, can cause serious health consequences to our pets.

From the International Journal of Food Microbiology, Drs. Herman J. Boermans and Maxwell C.K. Leung published the report *"Mycotoxins and the pet food industry: Toxicological evidence and risk assessment"* in 2007. This report gives pet owners a wealth of information on the risks associated with many common pet food ingredients, plus it more than proves the point that strict mycotoxin testing must be required of pet food manufacturers.

One of the biggest issues of concern discussed is that existing studies of mycotoxin contamination in pet food overlook the day to day consumption of small amounts of mycotoxins resulting in *"chronic diseases such as liver and kidney fibrosis, infections resulting from immunosuppression and cancer."* While practicing veterinarians are familiar with severe mycotoxin contamination symptoms in pets, Drs. Boermans and Leung suggest chronic diseases are *"often overlooked"* when caused by long term consumption of lesser amounts of mycotoxins.

The following are excerpts...

"These available reports of acute mycotoxicosis, however, cannot provide the whole picture of the mycotoxin problem associated with pet foods since only a small

number of food poisoning cases are published. Veterinarians, furthermore, often overlooked mycotoxins as the cause of chronic diseases such as liver and kidney fibrosis, infections resulting from immunosuppression and cancer. These findings suggest that mycotoxin contamination in pet food poses a serious health threat to pet species."

"Aflatoxins are commonly found in corn, peanuts, cottonseed, milk, and tree nuts. After ingestion, aflatoxins are absorbed and carried to the liver via the circulatory system. They are then converted by the liver into toxic reactive epoxides which bind covalently to intracellular macromolecules such as DNA, RNA and protein enzymes, resulting in damage to liver cells."

"In addition to their hepatotoxic properties, aflatoxins are also carcinogenic. The binding of DNA causes genotoxicity and mutation in cells. The chronic carcinogenic dose of aflatoxins is much lower than the acute dose. Since aflatoxins are both acute and chronic hepatotoxins and carcinogens, the actual number of dogs affected by aflatoxins would be far more than the total number reported in acute poisoning cases."

"Ochratoxins are a group of potent renal mycotoxins that widely contaminate the agricultural commodities, such as corn, wheat, oats and dried beans, in temperate regions. There are four ochratoxin homo-logues — A, B, C and D. Ochratoxin A (OTA) is the most prevalent and, together with ochratoxin C, most toxic. Initial symptoms of ochratoxicosis observed in all species include anorexia, polydipsia, polyuria and dehydration, and are associated with renal damage."

"Upon absorption, ochratoxins enter the circulatory system, bind tightly to serum proteins and accumulate in the kidneys, where they disrupt protein synthesis and other pathways in proximal tubular cells. This results in the degeneration of the proximal tubules and interstitial fibroses. OTA is also known to bind with DNA molecules and induce renal tumors in animal models, although its carcinogenic mechanism remains controversial. Dogs show a high susceptibility to OTA."

"Trichothecenes are a family of Fusarium mycotoxins commonly found in corn, wheat, barley, as well as oats worldwide. Trichothecenes are potent irritants and inhibitors of protein and DNA synthesis which interfere with cellular metabolic activities, ultimately leading to cell death. Rapidly dividing cells are particularly sensitive with the gastrointestinal and immune systems primarily affected in exposed animals. Typical clinical signs of trichothecene toxicosis include loss of appetite, vomiting, diarrhea, gastrointestinal hemorrhage, ataxia, and immune suppression."

"Feed refusal and vomiting, the most notable behavioral effects of trichothecenes, are possibly related to their influences on brain regional neurochemistry and feed intake regulation. The vulnerability of gastrointestinal and immune systems to trichothecene toxicity accounts for the symptoms of gastrointestinal distress, bloody diarrhea and immune suppression in trichothecene poisoning."

"Multiple mycotoxin exposure is common in the natural situation. The toxicity of a particular mycotoxin, therefore, depends on not only its own concentration but also the presence of other mycotoxins. Thus mycotoxins of relatively low toxicity may pose significant risks if exposure is great, frequent, and long. Although the exposure of pet animals to mycotoxins in grain-based pet food is generally low, it is unavoidable and occurs throughout the entire lifespan of the animal."

"Mycotoxin contamination in pet food poses a serious health threat to pets. The health problems of pets are of a highly emotional concern and pet food safety is the responsibility of the pet food industry. Risk and safety determination is needed and must address many issues including sensitivity of toxic endpoints, multiple mycotoxin exposure, and pet food amelioration." (31)

My interpretation of this paper suggests that pet owners avoid pet foods/treats containing grains common to mycotoxin contamination. The ingredients most frequently mentioned were corn and wheat; to a lesser extent (mentioned in the paper) were barley and oats. Because we pet owners don't know the testing methods each pet food manufacturer follows on mycotoxin testing or what allowable levels they accept in ingredients or the long term effect of day to day minute mycotoxin consumption, avoiding these ingredients seems to be our only recourse. The paper also suggested the addition of antioxidants (berries are a great source) and omega-3 polyunsaturated fatty acids (fish oil a great source - should be purified grade) to the diet helped to protect the pet from mycotoxin exposure. Add berries and fish oil to your pets food just in case!

Canola Oil

Many different brands of dog foods and cat foods have chosen to use canola oil in their products; several even utilize the heart-healthy claim provided to canola oil by the FDA. However, a great deal of research shows canola oil is anything but healthy.

The Weston A. Price Foundation, calls canola *'The Great Con-ola'*. (32) Authors Sally Fallon and Mary G. Enig, Ph.D. report that canola oil was developed because industry needed a cheap source of monounsaturated oils. In the 1980's, the world was beginning to learn the health benefits of olive oil, yet for industry, there was not enough olive oil in the world to meet need, and olive oil was too expensive to use in most processed foods.

Rapeseed oil, predominately used in China, Japan and India, was a monounsaturated oil option. However, two-thirds of the fatty acids in rapeseed oil are *"erucic acid"*, associated with Keshan's disease causing lesions of the heart. Canadian plant breeders developed a genetic manipulation of rape seed that greatly reduced the erucic acid. The new oil was introduced as LEAR oil for Low Erucic Acid Rapeseed.

Realizing neither 'rape' nor 'lear' would present a healthy image, industry dubbed the new oil canola for Canadian oil (most of the new genetically modified rapeseed at the time was grown in Canada). Canada's Canola Council's initial challenge was rapeseed was not a GRAS (Generally Recognized as Safe) food in the US. FDA GRAS status was granted in 1985 for canola oil for which, it is rumored, the Canadian government spent $50 million to obtain.

The Weston A. Price Foundation article quotes numerous studies of the effects of canola oil in animals; *"These studies all point in the same direction-- that canola oil is definitely not healthy for the cardiovascular system. Like rapeseed oil, its predecessor, canola oil is associated with fibrotic lesions of the heart. It also causes vitamin E deficiency, undesirable changes in the blood platelets and shortened life-span in stroke-prone rats when it was the only oil in the animals' diet. Furthermore, it seems to retard growth, which is why the FDA does not allow the use of canola oil in infant formula."*

Journalist David Lawrence Dewey quotes research from the University of Florida that *"determined that as much as 4.6% of all the fatty acids in unrefined canola are 'trans' isomers (which are somewhat like plastic) due to the refining process."* (33)

Dewey also points out that canola oil is registered with the EPA as an approved pesticide. (34)

Despite an overwhelming amount of research, the FDA, provided the U.S. Canola Association the following health claim permission in October 2006: "*Limited and not conclusive scientific evidence suggests that eating about 1 ½ tablespoons (19 grams) of canola oil daily may reduce the risk of coronary heart disease due to the unsaturated fat content in canola oil. To achieve this possible benefit, canola oil is to replace a similar amount of saturated fat and not increase the total number of calories you eat in a day. One serving of this product contains [x] grams of canola oil.*" (35)

Why would pet food companies and human food companies promote canola oil as a healthy option? Authors Sally Fallon and Mary G. Enig answer this perfectly - "*payola for the food companies and con-ola for the public.*"

More on Canola

It is startling to see the number of pet foods and treats that are using canola oil. It is becoming the trend ingredient, so much so that it caused me to wonder if I had previously given canola oil a bad rap. A revisit to canola oil research provided me with no comfort but only concern as to why it is so commonly used in pet foods.

My previous article about canola oil quoted one of the most respected journalists of truth in health and nutrition, David Lawrence Dewey. Mr. Dewey had nothing good to say about canola. But, I went in search for more. Below is what I found.

A documented conversation of several medical experts published on the Journal of the American College of Nutrition website stated...

"*Canola oil is not allowed in infant formula in the United States or Canada. Some studies in humans have associated intake of canola oil with cardiac fatty infiltration. More recently, some studies using hypertensive rats have shown that intake of canola oil increases hypertensive events in these animals.*" (36)

In a Japanese study of rats fed a diet containing canola oil..."*These results indicate that promotion of hypertension-related deterioration in organs is likely to have relevance to the short life span in the canola oil group.*" (37)

In another study published in The Journal of Nutrition "*Vegetable oils contain various minor components such as fat-soluble vitamins, phytosterols, isoflavonoids, tocopherols, and environmental chemicals. Fat-soluble substances are generally secreted into breast milk and are likely to affect the pups' physiology. The spontaneously hypertensive rat, stroke prone (SHRSP) strain, derived from the SHR and Wistar-Kyoto (WKY) strains, develops hypertension and dies of stroke frequently, particularly when salt is added to their drinking water. SHRSP rats exhibit various other anomalies such as renal injury, peroxidative injury, developmental disorders, and reproductive physiologic disorders. Using this strain, we showed that dietary perilla seed oil, flaxseed oil, and fish oil with very low (n-6)/(n-3) ratios prolong survival by 10% compared with safflower and soybean oils with high (n-6)/(n-3) ratios; however, canola oil (Can), with a relatively low (n-6)/(n-3) ratio (2.5), markedly shortens survival (40% in the absence of NaCl in the drinking water) compared with soybean oil (Soy).*" (38)

Another concern I found were numerous (brief) statements on possible allergic reactions in humans to canola on which no studies have been performed (never the less no studies on dogs and cats allergen potential).

So to make a long story short(er), I remain steadfast believing that canola oil has no place in pet food. It is a genetically modified (GM) oil, and there is no research on the safety of its use in pet foods and treats. Yes, there is a multitude of science that shows positive benefits of canola, but one thing remains very troubling to me...

If the FDA does not allow the use of canola oil in infant formula, there has got to be a mighty big reason why not. Though it might be simple, my logic is that if canola oil is not safe for human babies to consume in their food, then it's not safe for my furry babies to consume in food. Until there is sound scientific research proving canola oil is 100% safe and beneficial to dogs and cats, it will remain a red flag ingredient for me regardless of how many pet food manufacturers think it's trendy!

Food Dyes

The Center for Science in the Public Interest (CSPI) has published a informative report on the risk of food dyes. CSPI states many currently approved dyes raise health concerns.

Many pet foods and treats include dyes merely to please the eye of the consumer. The pets don't care what color the food or treat is and can't see the colors anyway. While research on risks of dyes in food is primarily done to show risks to humans, these studies are done on laboratory animals. Thus negative results prove dyes are a risk to the dogs and cats consuming them in foods and treats.

Of the common food dyes found in pet foods and treats, the CSPI summary states...

"*Blue 2 cannot be considered safe given the statistically significant incidence of tumors, particularly brain gliomas, in male rats. It should not be used in foods.*"

"*Red 40, the most widely used dye, may accelerate the appearance of immune system tumors in mice. The dye causes hyper-sensitivity (allergy-like) reactions in a small number of consumers and might trigger hyperactivity in children. Considering the safety questions and its non-essentiality, Red 40 should be excluded from foods unless and until new tests clearly demonstrate its safety.*"

"*Yellow 5 was not carcinogenic in rats but was not adequately tested in mice. It may be contaminated with several cancer-causing chemicals. In addition, Yellow 5 causes sometimes severe hypersensitivity reactions in a small number of people and might trigger hyperactivity and other behavior effects in children. Posing some risks while serving no nutritional or safety purpose, Yellow 5 should not be allowed in foods.*"

"*Yellow 6 caused adrenal tumors in animals, though that is disputed by industry and the FDA. It may be contaminated with cancer-causing chemicals and occasionally causes severe hypersensitivity reactions. Yellow 6 adds an unnecessary risk to the food supply.*"

Needless to say, read the ingredients of your pet food and treats and avoid all that contain dyes.

GMO

The Center for Food Safety and The True Food Network works "*to protect human health and the environment by curbing the proliferation of harmful food production technologies and by promoting organic and other forms of sustainable agriculture."* (39)

These organizations have put together a *"shoppers' guide"* to help consumers find and avoid GE ingredients in food. Basically, consumers need to avoid corn products (including corn oil, corn syrup, high fructose corn syrup, corn starch, corn meal), soy products (soy protein, soy lecithin, soy oil, soy sauce, soy isolates), canola (canola oil), and cotton (cottonseed oil). The number one tip suggested to consumers is to *"Buy Organic"*.

But what about pet food? How can pet owners avoid GMO ingredients in their pets' food?

Avoid the same four basic foods, corn, soy, canola, and cotton. The following is a list of common pet food ingredients which could be (probably are) genetically modified and are recommended to be avoided in your pet's food and treats:

Corn
Ground corn
Ground yellow corn
Whole corn
Whole grain ground corn
Corn gluten
Corn gluten meal
Corn starch-modified
Dried fermented corn extractives
Corn germ meal

Soy
Soybean hulls
Soybean meal
Soybean oil
Soy flour
Soy protein concentrate

Canola oil

More on GM

Shocking but not surprising results from a study on Monsanto's genetically modified (GM) corn reveals side effects associated with kidney and liver disease. Research data for the study was obtained from Monsanto by European governments and Greenpeace, then analyzed by numerous scientists.

Monsanto's own data, given up only because of their loss of a court action, was analyzed by scientists. The team of scientists not only discovered Monsanto's poor testing procedures but they also discovered numerous risk results from rats consuming GM corn.

"Effects were mostly concentrated in kidney and liver function, the two major diet detoxification organs, but in detail differed with each GM type. In addition, some effects on heart, adrenal, spleen and blood cells were also frequently noted. As there normally exists sex differences in liver and kidney metabolism, the highly statistically significant disturbances in the function of these organs, seen between male and female rats, cannot be dismissed as biologically insignificant as has been proposed by others. We therefore conclude that our data strongly suggests that these GM maize varieties induce a state of hepatorenal toxicity. This can be due to the new pesticides (herbicides or insecticides) present specifically in each type of GM maize, although unintended metabolic effects due to the mutagenic properties of the GM transformation process cannot be excluded. Our analysis highlights the kidneys and liver as particularly important on which to focus such research as there was a clear negative impact on the function of these organs in rats consuming GM maize varieties for just 90 days." (40)

Which pet foods/treats use GM corn (grains)? We don't know. I won't even bother to ask the pet food companies, I'm confident they won't tell me. The best advice I can give you is to avoid any corn ingredient in any pet product (food, treat, litter).

Arsenic in Animal Food

This is one of those ridiculous but true stories. Arsenic, the deadly poison and known carcinogen, is an allowed ingredient in some animal feed.

The Alliance for Natural Health reports that last December, the Center for Food Safety and the Institute for Agriculture and Trade Policy filed a petition with the FDA asking for the removal of arsenic-containing compounds used in animal feeds. "*Most arsenic-containing animal feed additives are not used to treat sickness. Instead, these additives are commonly used in poultry production to induce faster weight gain and give the meat a healthy-looking color; the same techniques are used to a lesser extent in turkeys and hogs.*" (41)

In 2006, the Institute for Agriculture and Trade Policy published a startling paper titled "*Playing Chicken, Avoiding Arsenic in your Meat*". While the U.S. Department of Agriculture (USDA) claims that none or very little of the arsenic put into chicken feed makes its way into the meat, this organization tested raw chicken purchased from supermarkets and fried chicken purchased from fast food chains. They found that most uncooked chicken products (55%) contained "*detectable arsenic*" and many fast food chickens "*carried some detectable arsenic*" as well. (This is a very fascinating and well written report.) (42)

There is no available information of arsenic levels in chicken meat used in pet foods. Because many pets eat chicken-based food and eat that food every day of their lives (unlike humans who might only consume chicken two or three times a week), this is a huge concern for pet owners. If a pet food does or does not contain arsenic depends on the chicken producer the pet food company purchases from. My guess would be few, if any, pet food companies test for arsenic levels in their chicken or chicken meal. However, again considering that many pets eat chicken-based pet food day in and day out for years, this should be a consideration for all conscientious pet food companies. So if you pet food companies are listening out there, please test for arsenic levels and provide those test results on your website.

For pet owners who feed raw or home-cooked food with chicken to your pets, the above Institute for Agriculture and Trade Policy paper lists the raw chicken companies they tested and levels of arsenic found.

Ethoxyquin

Ethoxyquin is an ugly word in my book. It's even uglier because of what some pet food companies are telling pet owners about 'e'. Don't believe everything pet food manufacturers tell you.

Ethoxyquin is a chemical preservative linked to serious disease. I have very personal negative feelings about this chemical because it killed my dog 18 years ago. My very wise veterinarian back then educated me that my Samantha's (Sam's) bone cancer was more than likely caused by this chemical. I will never forget the heartache when he told me and I will never forget what the pet food company (at the time, the leading U.S. pet food manufacturer) told me either. My veterinarian educated me that 'e' was commonly used to extend the shelf life of pet food. The pet food company told me the shelf life of this highly popular dog food was 25 years! No kidding. My dog died at 8 years old but her food would stay fresh for 17 more years thanks to 'e'!

Developed by Monsanto, ethoxyquin is rarely used or allowed in human foods today. Some spices are allowed by the FDA to be preserved with ethoxyquin. Sadly, the chemical is still used in some pet treats and to preserve fish meal ingredients in some pet foods. If 'e' or any other preservative is used by a supplier of ingredients to a pet food, 'e' will not be listed on your pet food label. The only way to know is to call the pet food manufacturer and ask and hope to receive a truthful answer. Thus, the problem.

After the first of a series of 'e' articles was published on TruthaboutPetFood.com, varied responses about pet food came rolling in from pet owners.

The following was recently sent to me. This was posted in a pet forum by the pet owner....

"I just spent quite some time on the phone with XXXXXXX, the pet food I use, and the customer rep was quite knowledgeable about the ethoxyquin issue. Basically, she has the FDA 2010 guidelines right in front of her and ethoxyquin is still the ONLY FDA approved preservative for fish meal being supplied to the US. She says Natorox* is approved in Canada but not in the US. XXXXXXX has been trying to get around this for some time because they would like to eliminate ethoxyquin from their food altogether and they have not had any luck getting FDA to approve allowing a supplier to provide fish meal preserved with Naturox as of this time. They are still trying. Their suggestion in the meantime was that there are several formulas that do not have fish in the ingredients. She was so straightforward with me on this issue that I have to believe

her on the FDA approvals, and perhaps the person writing about the ethoxyquin was misinformed about the FDA approval of Naturox."

Ok…just because a customer service representative of a pet food company is nice doesn't mean they are giving you the whole story or being honest. This pet owner doesn't have to believe me. She can spend a few minutes doing some research and learn the truth for herself.

This pet food company just bold-faced lied to this pet owner.

*Naturox, manufactured by Kemin Industries, is already approved by U. S. federal regulations. No additional permit or application is needed (I assume that it is approved for use in Canada, but I am certain it is approved for use in the U.S. right now.). Any fish meal supplier can purchase Naturox, receive proper instruction from Kemin Industries on use, application, and storage. There is no shortage of Naturox (another popular excuse heard from pet food – a shortage of naturally-preserved meal). Any pet food manufacturer can insist that the meal be preserved with Naturox by their suppliers or they can continue using 'e' and lie to their customers!

Again, Naturox is a natural preservative alternative to ethoxyquin already approved by U.S. federal regulations. This pet food company is telling customers they have no other option. Well then, how can so many other pet food companies whose product is made and sold in the U.S. be using Naturox-preserved fish meal ingredients? Others use Naturox because it IS approved for use in the U.S. and they don't wish to feed their customers' pets 'e'.

Any pet food company can use 'e'-preserved fish meal if they want to but if they do, it is unethical to mislead (lie to) their customers. The truth does come out. We are watching!

More on 'E'
One pet food company has told pet owners that their fish meal is 'e' free, yet supposedly they provide test results showing 5 ppm of 'e' in their fish meal. Another pet food company is telling pet owners about pet food #1's claim to be 'e' free and that there is a shortage of 'e' free fish meal. And then there's the claim that the 'e' is cooked out during the pet food manufacturing process and that naturally preserved fish meals (using

Naturox or natural tocopherols) is causing an alarming rate of peroxide levels in fish meal. Thus, it is more harmful than 'e'. Hmmm... Here's what I found out.

Ethoxyquin is a chemical preservative used in some pet food/treats directly and indirectly. 'E' used directly would be listed in the pet product ingredients. Used indirectly, it would not be listed on the pet food/treat label. Pet food regulations allow pet food/treat companies the privilege of NOT including ingredients that were added by ingredient suppliers. As an example, fish meal is a very common pet food ingredient. Many fish meal suppliers use 'e' as a preservative in the fish meal sold to pet food/treat manufacturers. Because the manufacturer did not add the 'e' to the manufacturing (the ingredient supplier did), 'e' would not be required to be listed on the pet food/treat label.

First off, ethoxyquin was developed by Monsanto. In 2007, Greg Aldrich, PhD (Pet Food Industry Consultant, Journalist to PetFoodIndustry.com) reported on the Pet Food Industry website that in the 1980's there were a *"number of anecdotal reports to the Food and Drug Administration (FDA) by pet owners of reproductive problems, cancer, itchy skin, etc. in their pets."* Dr. Aldrich states that most of these claims have been refuted, thanks to additional studies provided by Monsanto (Yes, additional studies performed by Monsanto! The manufacturer was trusted.). The FDA has basically dropped the issue of ethoxyquin concern since. (43)

Today, I discovered no mention of 'e' on the Monsanto website. However, I did find on ChemicalBook.com a list of six suppliers of 'e', each one of them based in China. Safety data from Chemicalbook.com states ethoxyquin is harmful if swallowed and urges that contact with skin be avoided. It is assigned the Hazard Code Xn – hazardous. (44)

Ethoxyquin is registered with the EPA for use as an antioxidant to control scald (browning) in pears. 'E' is also regulated by the FDA for its use as a preservative in animal feed, dehydrated crops and sorghum, and as an antioxidant for the preservation of color in the production of chili powder, paprika, and ground chili. The EPA admits there is limited information on the risk of 'e' and states that what we do know provides enough information *"for the limited use of this chemical."* (45)

Although federal regulations state that 'e' must be used as a preservative on fish meal entering the United States, ANY fish meal supplier can opt for an approved safer preservative with full government approval. One such safer preservative is Naturox (used by many pet food companies). I spoke with Jim Mann of Kemin Industries, the manufacturer of Naturox.

Unlike what some pet food companies are telling pet owners, Kemin Industries shared that there is no shortage of Naturox. Thus there would be no shortage of naturally preserved fish meal should any supplier wish to use Naturox versus 'e'. Fish IS a seasonal product, but no more seasonal than many other products commonly used in pet food. Because Naturox is already approved for use on fish meal entering the US, no fish meal provider or pet food company would need to apply for any costly and/or time consuming permits. Kemin works closely with fish meal suppliers providing instructions for proper use of Naturox and proper storage of the meal. Which leads me to...

Again, unlike what some pet food companies are telling pet owners, Kemin Industries told me that a fish meal preserved naturally would NOT be more likely to have higher peroxide levels, "*not if it's managed properly.*" Mismanagement of fish meal would include improper application of ANY preservative and improper storage. Quoting one pet food manufacturer, "*Also, the peroxide levels are much higher than we feel comfortable with. Peroxide is an indicator of oxidation. Peroxide can cause vomiting and may even cause damage to vital organs.*" Yes, peroxide is an indicator of oxidation as well as an indicator of mismanaged fish meal. Mismanaged fish meal with higher peroxide levels resulting in a risk to pets can occur with ANY preservative, including 'e'. It is not indicative of natural preservatives as pet owners are being told.

One more note about 'e' that pet food has neglected to mention. ChemicalBook.com states "*Ethoxyquin may undergo a hazardous polymerization at temperatures above 320 degrees F. Tends to polymerize and darken in color on exposure to light and air. Not compatible with oxidizing agents and with strong acids.*" (46)

Thus, if any pet food containing 'e' is heated above 320 F, a hazardous chain reaction could very well alter the entire pet food/treat. Since many pet food/treat companies claim cooking temperatures are 'proprietary', even if 'e' is listed on the label (instead of hidden within an ingredient itself), pet owners have no idea if 'e' has damaged the food/treat in a 'hazardous' way.

Why some pet food manufacturers are telling pet owners their fish meal is 'e' free, yet they state their meal analysis at less than 5 ppm, is confusing. Ethoxyquin is NOT naturally found in fish. It would be discovered at any part per million ONLY if the chemical was added somewhere along the processing line.

Don't believe everything pet food tells you. Do your research. If you are lied to by a pet food company, that should be a very clear sign of the quality of the food/treat this company produces.

Propylene Glycol

Although it is on the FDA's GRAS (Generally Recognized as Safe) list, many other experts don't have much good to say about the safety of propylene glycol. What is this ingredient and why is it in some foods and treats?

The FDA states propylene glycol is used as a humectant in soft-moist pet foods which helps retain water and gives these products their unique texture and taste. Basically, propylene glycol is used as a preservative to soft-moist pet foods and treats. From the FDA website: *"It was affirmed Generally Recognized As Safe (GRAS) for use in human and animal food before the advent of soft-moist foods. It was known for some time that propylene glycol caused Heinz Body formation (small clumps of proteins seen in the cells when viewed under the microscope) in the red blood cells of cats, but it could not be shown to cause overt anemia or other clinical effects. However, reports in the veterinary literature of scientifically sound studies have shown that propylene glycol reduces the red blood cell survival time, renders red blood cells more susceptible to oxidative damage, and has other adverse effects in cats consuming the substance at levels found in soft-moist food. In light of these new data, CVM amended the regulations to expressly prohibit the use of propylene glycol in cat foods."* (47)

Wikipedia provides the following information for the safety of propylene glycol in animals: *"Veterinary data indicates that propylene glycol is toxic to 50% of dogs at doses of 9mL/kg, although the figure is higher for most laboratory*

81

animals (LD50 at levels of 20mL/kg). However, propylene glycol may be toxic to cats in ways not seen in other animals. The U.S. Food and Drug Administration has determined that its presence in or on cat food has not been shown by adequate scientific data to be safe for use. Any such use is considered an adulteration of the cat food and a violation of the Federal Food, Drug, and Cosmetic Act." (48)

The Material Safety Data Sheet from the Department of Commerce provides the following warning regarding ingestion of propylene glycol: *"May cause gastrointestinal irritation with nausea, vomiting and diarrhea. Low hazard for usual industrial handling. May cause emoglobinuric nephrosis. May cause changes in surface EEG."* (49)

Most scientific data on the safety of propylene glycol is based on use in cosmetics and human skin conditioning products. Environmental Working Group's Skin Deep section (a cosmetic safety database) states their researchers reviewed available research and found that this ingredient is linked to cancer, developmental/reproductive toxicity, allergies, and skin, eye, and lung irritation. Again in relation to skin, EWG gave the ingredient a 'moderate hazard' rating. (50)

Carrageenan

It's one of the many ingredients found on the label of some pet foods. What is it? Is it safe? Here is a close look at the common pet food ingredient carrageenan.

TLC Cooking gave the perfect introduction to explaining why carrageenan is used in pet food. *"Lots of foods can contain some pretty weird-sounding stuff. That's because processed foods have some amazing things they have to do. For example, a cookie might get made in Texas, trucked across the country in the middle of the summer, sit in a warehouse for a couple of weeks before it is sold and then ride home in the trunk of your car. And when you open the package, you expect the cookie to look perfect. Not an easy thing to accomplish, it turns out."* (51)

Many foods, including pet foods, include chemicals known as gums such as carrageenan. Gums help to thicken and emulsify (help liquids stay mixed) foods. Carrageenan is a seaweed extract. So…is it safe in pet food?

In *"Review of harmful gastrointestinal effects of carrageenan in animal experiments"* by J. K. Tobacman from the College of Medicine, University of Iowa, carrageenan doesn't get a very good (safe) review. *"Review of these data demonstrated that exposure to undegraded as well as to degraded carrageenan was associated with the occurrence of intestinal ulcerations and neoplasms."* In 1972, the FDA *"considered restricting dietary carrageenan ...this resolution did not prevail, and no subsequent regulation has restricted use."* In 1982, the International Agency for Research on Cancer identified *"sufficient evidence for the carcinogenicity of degraded carrageenan in animals to regard it as posing a carcinogenic risk to humans."* (52)

From the International Agency for Research on Cancer, carrageenan is rated *"2B: Possibly carcinogenic to humans"*. (53)

From the website NotMilk.com, an educational website from the Dairy Education Board, Executive Directory Robert Cohen has some very negative things to say about carrageenan. His article states, *"Carrageenan is a commonly used food additive that is extracted from red seaweed by using powerful alkali solvents. These solvents would remove the tissues and skin from your hands as readily as would any acid."* When addressing whether carrageenan is natural, this author states *"Carrageenan is about as wholesome as monosodium glutamate (MSG), which is extracted from rice and can equally be considered natural. Just because something comes from a natural source does not mean that it is safe. The small black dots in the eyes of potatoes contain substances that are instantly fatal if eaten. Got poison? You will if you eat the black dots on the "eyes" of potatoes."*

Although much of Dr. Tobacman's research on carrageenan was based on human tissue, much of the research she quotes is from animal studies. Thus, we can safely assume that carrageenan is not an ingredient we want to see listed on a pet food label.

Wheat Gluten Meat in Canned Pet Foods

Have you ever wondered how a can of dog food or cat food that includes chunks of meat only costs $0.89? The secret to the low price is in the chunks.

A popular brand of dog food boasts 'choice' and 'cuts' on the label. Its beef flavored. The label of the can shows a picture of large chunks of raw meat as well as what appears to be the cooked chunks of meat. However, it only costs $0.89 for a 13.2 ounce can. How can they do that? Open a can of dog food or cat food, dump it onto a plate, and you've got a plate full of meat, right? Maybe not.

Actual Canned Dog Food

The above picture is of this grocery store brand dog food, about 1/3 of the can on a plate. The 13.2 ounce large can costs $0.89.

This photo of the dog food label clearly shows 'chunks' of lean raw meat along with the cooked version of the dog food. The words 'Cuts' and 'Beef' are boldly stated on the label.

Actual Dog Food Label

This $0.89 can of dog food, which appears to contain chunks of meat in gravy, breaks down to $0.07 per ounce and $1.12 per pound. A can of beef (people food) in natural juices from Internet Grocer costs $0.46 per ounce or $7.36 per pound. (54)

Many pet owners believe without question that the 'chunks' are meat in these dog foods. The thought of why it would cost a mere $0.89 for a 13.2 ounce can doesn't even enter their consciousness, perhaps justifiably so because of the dog food label pictures and wording on the label. However, the truth is that this dog food, which appears to be a can full of chunks of cooked beef, has very little beef in it at all.

The little understood secret of pet food is that the 'chunks' are NOT actual chunks of meat. They are ground up animal parts (perhaps rejected for use in human food) glued together with wheat glutens to make the appearance of chunks of meat. The chunks in some pet food (certainly in this $0.89 can of dog food) are not chunks of meat and they may or may not contain any actual meat.

The ingredients of this dog food, along with the cost, should tell a pet owner the true story. Ingredients…"*water, chicken, meat by-products, wheat flour, beef, wheat gluten…*"

Important things to notice about these ingredients:
• Chicken is listed higher on the ingredient list than beef. Yet the food is a beef dog food.

• Ingredient chicken is the entire bird (less head, feet, and entrails). It may or may not be human grade, includes bones and internal organs. The 'chicken' is ground whole. Thus the chunks cannot be chicken meat.

• Meat by-products can be the discarded left-overs from any animal. By definition, this is not meat and is not human grade. Again, ingredient is ground. Chunks cannot be chicken meat.

• There is more wheat flour, by weight, in this can of dog food than beef! Yet the food is named 'Beef'. (Do you realize how much flour it takes to weigh more than meat?)

So, the chicken, meat by-products, and beef are finely ground, toss in a great deal of wheat flour and wheat gluten to glue it all together, and press the concoction into chunks. Presto!... pretend meat chunks to confuse (or mislead, depending on how you look at it) unknowing pet owners!

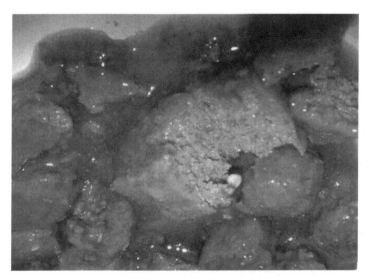

Close up of a 'chunk' cut apart

When you look at the chunk closely, it has the appearance of meat loaf (I prefer to call it mystery meat loaf).

This pet food, a 'beef' pet food, contains more chicken, by-products, and flour than beef. The photograph on the product label shows choice cuts of raw beef along with a picture similar to the 'cooked' chunks shown above, greatly implying that the 'chunks' are cooked beef. The product label also states 'cuts'; again, implying cuts of meat are included in this food. The chunks probably contain only a very small portion of actual meat. The dogs that consume this food are eating lots of flour and gluten. This can of Beef Cuts in Gravy dog food sells for $0.07 an ounce versus $0.46 an ounce for human grade canned beef in natural juices.

By the way, these types of tricks happen every single day with pet foods. If human food manufacturers did the same, advertising regulations would stop them immediately. Food, Drug and Cosmetic Act laws clearly state that any food label, human or pet, is NOT allowed to mislead the consumer.

While some canned dog foods and cat foods actually DO contain slices or chunks of USDA human grade beef or chicken, many others only imply they do. Read the pet food ingredient label. If you see flour and gluten ingredients, and/or if the can costs far less than what any meat costs today, you can guess the 'chunks' are not meat.

Flouride

As if pet owners don't have enough things to worry about with their pet food, now we have to be concerned about high levels of fluoride in pet food. Environmental Working Group (EWG) just released a new study that showed high levels of fluoride in eight of ten pet foods tested.

Fluoride would be the last thing you would think of when selecting a dog food or cat food! However when you consider the latest study published by EWG, fluoride contamination appears to be a risk with some pet foods. *"Eight of ten dog food brands tested by an independent laboratory commissioned by Environmental Working Group (EWG) contain fluoride in amounts up to 2.5 times higher than the Environmental Protection Agency's (EPA) national drinking water standard."* (55)

Veterinary science has not studied safe levels of fluoride for dogs or cats. However, people who consume excessive fluoride *"often develop mottled teeth (dental fluorosis) and weakened bones, leading to more fractures. High fluoride consumption is also associated with reproductive and developmental system damage, neurotoxicity, hormonal disruption and bone cancer (NRC 2006)."*

The EWG report states: *"Fluoride occurs naturally in some water supplies. But two-thirds of Americans -- and their pets and live-stock-- drink water that has been artificially fluoridated on grounds it improves dental health. Fluoride is also found in certain foods, those from plants grown in high-fluoride soils or those to which the chemical is introduced during processing. Once ingested with food or water, fluoride accumulates in the bones. An average dog who drinks adequate water daily would be exposed to 0.05 to 0.1 milligrams of fluoride per kilogram of body weight, depending on the dog's weight and water consumption. But those dogs who eat food high in fluoride, day in and day out, may be exposed to unsafe levels of fluoride. For example, a 10-pound puppy that eats about a cup of dog food a day would consume 0.25 milligrams of fluoride per kilogram of body weight per day, an amount five times higher than the "safe" level set by the Agency for Toxic Substances and Disease Registry (ATSDR) of the U.S. Department of Health and Human Services."*

EWG concluded that the ingredients common to the high levels of fluoride in dog food include *"chicken by-product meal"*, *"poultry by-product meal"*, *"chicken meal"*, *"beef and bone meal"*.

The EWG report mistakenly states the above ingredients are *"basically ground bones, cooked with steam, dried, and mashed to make a cheap dog food filler."* This statement is incorrect. The pet food ingredient 'chicken meal' is NOT 'basically cooked ground bones'. Some pet food manufacturers include muscle meat, internal organs and bones in their chicken meal while others use muscle meat ONLY in their chicken meal.

It is assumed from the EWG report that the conclusion derived from this study is that by-products (some internal organs are defined as by-products) and bone meals are the source of high fluoride levels in dog foods. Although cat foods were not studied by EWG, it is assumed that cats are subject to the same risks of high fluoride levels in some cat foods. Dog food and cat food ingredients that could contain high levels of fluoride (based on EWG's findings) are: chicken by-product meal, poultry by-product meal, meat meal, meat and bone meal, animal digest, and chicken meal when the manufacturer includes bones and/or internal organs in chicken meal.

To limit your pet's risk of excessive amounts of fluoride, avoid pet foods that contain the above mentioned ingredients. Again, please note, the ingredient chicken meal should only be a risk ingredient (per the EWG report) if the ingredient contains bones and/or internal organs. If you have any doubt if the pet food ingredient chicken meal used in your pet's food contains bones and/or internal organs, call or email the manufacturer.

Fluoride water filters are available. However, they are pricey and your search needs to be specific to filter fluoride from the water. As an example, a Brita water filter does NOT filter fluoride.

BPA

The Harvard School of Public Health just released a new study confirming the risk of BPA (bisphenol A), a chemical common to plastic and canned pet and human foods. Participants in the Harvard study showed a two-thirds increase of BPA in their urine. Exposure to BPA has been scientifically linked to cardiovascular disease and diabetes.

The FDA continues to stand firm on the side of big industry with BPA. Existing FDA regulations continue to allow BPA in everything from baby bottles to pet food can linings. On the flip side of the FDA, modern research, including the latest study from Harvard, continues to show the risks of BPA. *"We found that drinking cold liquids from polycarbonate bottles for just one week increased urinary BPA levels by more than two-thirds. If you heat those bottles, as is the case with baby bottles, we would expect the levels to be considerably higher,"* states Karin Michels of Harvard. The 'heat' issue with canned dog and cat food is of huge concern for pet owners.

Canning is a method of preserving food. The canning process often heats the pet food after it is 'canned' to high temperatures. (56) Thus, pet food cans containing BPA in the lining are believed to contain higher levels of BPA that have leeched into the dog food or cat food, exposing the pet to serious health risks.

The Harvard study press release confirms the above belief. *"One of the study's strengths, the authors note, is that the students drank from the bottles in a normal use setting. Additionally, the students did not wash their bottles in dishwashers or put hot liquids in them; heating has been shown to increase the leaching of BPA from polycarbonate, so BPA levels might have been higher had students drunk hot liquids from the bottles."* (57)

Thankfully, there are some pet food manufacturers that are well aware of the risk of BPA in pet food can linings. These conscientious pet food makers use cans that do not contain a BPA lining. At this time, only small pet food cans are available without BPA in the lining. Some manufacturers ONLY sell canned foods in the small size because of the BPA risk. They do not even make or offer pet food in the larger BPA-lined can. Do not assume that all small cans of dog food or cat food do not contain BPA. It varies from manufacturer to manufacturer. If you provide your dog or cat with canned food, please contact the manufacturer and ask if their cans contain BPA or bisphenol A in the can lining. You could be saving your pet from serious disease by doing so.

David Case, journalist for FastCompany.com, recently published news on a BPA research investigation. His article is one of the most startling yet on the politics involved with BPA safety and/or risk.

The National Toxicology Program, part of the National Institutes of Health, reports there is 'some concern' regarding the safety of BPA. The FDA has decided the 'current levels of exposure' of BPA are safe. David Case of FastCompany.com went on a research journey to discover the truth of BPA himself.

Case discovered just five companies make BPA in the U.S. - *"Bayer, Dow, Hexion Specialty Chemicals, SABIC Innovative Plastics (formerly GE Plastics), and Sunoco. Together, they bring in more than $6 billion a year from the compound."* All of these corporations referred his questions of BPA safety to their trade association, the American Chemistry Council. The response from the American Chemistry Council was weak and evasive. *"Our view would be, Well, no, there isn't anything to be concerned about,"* says Steve Hentges, the council's point person on BPA. *"In a sense, you could have 'some concern' about just about anything."*

Case discovered that in more than 100 independently funded experiments on BPA, about 90% found evidence of adverse health effects at levels similar to typical human exposure. On the other hand, every industry-funded study conducted, a total of 14, found no risk effects.

When you read Case's article, you'll have no doubts about the risks of BPA. The problem is, when is the FDA going to do something about it?

Selenium

Read the fine print of many pet foods and you'll find the ingredient sodium selenite. More than 90% of pet foods include sodium selenite in their recipes. The other pet foods have chosen a safer alternative. Why? What follows is everything you wanted to know about selenium but probably didn't know you should ask.

Selenium is an essential element necessary in trace amounts in the diet of humans and animals. Fish, meat, poultry, whole grains, and dairy products are typical sources of this nutrient in the human diet. AAFCO and the FDA approve a selenium supplement to animal diets, most commonly in the form of sodium selenite for pet foods. Although it sounds simple enough, there is far more to the selenium story.

The Journal of the American College of Nutrition reports that not much was known about which selenium compounds to approve for use in animal feeds when the decisions were made back in the 1970's. *"At the time the regulatory action was taken, only the inorganic selenium salts (sodium selenite and sodium selenate) were available at a cost permitting their use in animal feed."* (58)

Science has since learned that these inorganic selenium sources (sodium selenite is most commonly used in pet foods) can be toxic in high doses affecting an animal's blood, liver, and muscles. The organic selenium yeast, on the other hand, has proven to be far less toxic, even in large doses. *"A study with rats showed that high doses (1.5 and 3.0 mg/kg body weight) of organic selenium in selenium yeast did not have any toxic effects after 14 days. This level of selenium is much higher than the theoretical toxic level for inorganic selenium."* (59)

So far, just to recap...selenium is a necessary element of a pet's diet. Furthermore, selenium yeast has proven to be a safe delivery method of selenium to our pets in their food. Knowing this, why is the possibly toxic sodium selenite the most popular delivery method of selenium in more than 90% of pet foods?

The selenium plot thickens. Backing up a bit, Eco-USA explains that selenium is a *"naturally occurring substance that is widely but unevenly distributed in the earth's crust and is commonly found in sedimentary rock. Selenium is not often found in its pure form but is usually combined with other substances. Much of the selenium in rocks is combined with sulfide minerals or with silver, copper, lead, and nickel minerals. When rocks change to soils, the selenium combines with oxygen to form several substances, the most common of which are sodium selenite and sodium selenate."* Furthermore, in some parts of the US, the soil contains such high levels of non-organic sodium selenite that animals grazing on plants in these areas can be harmed. (60)

Why are plants and animals consuming varying amounts of sodium selenite a potential problem to pet food?

Common grains used in pet foods can have varying levels of sodium selenite depending on the soil in different areas of the U.S. A batch of pet food using grain grown in western states can have a much higher level of sodium selenite than grains grown in eastern states. Pet owners have no knowledge of how much sodium selenite is included with each grain ingredient in their pet's food.

Depending on the sodium selenite levels of grains fed to meat-producing animals (or by-product producing animals), and depending on added sodium selenite levels of commercial feeds provided to these meat or by-product producing animals, every meat ingredient and by-product ingredient can vary in levels of selenium.

Add to the potential toxic build up the actual sodium selenite supplement added directly into your pet's food.

If all the wrong pieces of the puzzle fall into the wrong place, your pet's food, the result can be toxic.

"Humans who have accidentally eaten large amounts of selenium had upset stomachs, muscular weakness, difficulty in breathing, and pulmonary edema. Information about the health effects from eating or drinking too much selenium over long periods of

time has come from areas in China with very high selenium levels in the soil and in the rice and vegetables people eat. These people had loss of hair, loss of and poorly formed nails, problems with walking, reduced reflexes, and some paralysis when exposed to levels of 1.64 ppm or higher selenium in their food over months to years." (60)

ScienceLab.com states sodium selenite *"may be toxic to blood, kidneys, liver, skin, central nervous system. Repeated or prolonged exposure to the substance can produce target organ damage. Repeated exposure to a highly toxic material may produce general deterioration of health by an accumulation in one or many human organs."* (61)

The simple solution, as recent science has proven, seems to be adding non-toxic selenium yeast to animal feeds, including pet foods. *"Of about one dozen supplementation studies, none has shown evidence of toxicity even up to an intake level of 800 microg Se/d over a period of years. It is concluded that Se-yeast from reputable manufacturers is adequately characterized, of reproducible quality, and that there is no evidence of toxicity even at levels far above the EC tolerable upper intake level of 300 microg/d."* (62)

The FDA listened to research and approved selenium yeast to be used in chicken feed in 2000, cattle feed in 2007, and recently approved the safer selenium yeast for use in dog foods. There is no word from the FDA as to when approval for use of selenium yeast in cat foods will occur. I requested this information from the FDA on 3/24/08 and have received no response. There is no apparent excuse for the delay. Cat owners are urged to write the Center for Veterinary Management area of the FDA and (politely) encourage approval for use of selenium yeast in cat food.

Sadly, despite a wealth of research that proves sodium selenite can be toxic to animals including our pets, a large majority of pet food manufacturers continue to use sodium selenite instead of the scientifically proven safer alternative selenium yeast. Many pets could be suffering from an overdose of non-organic selenium without our knowledge.

Read the fine print of your pet's food ingredient list. Although it's a tiny ingredient, sodium selenite might not be an ingredient you want to be listed in your pet's food.

And then we learned more from a reader...

"Dear Susan,

You are on the right track with the selenium problem in food. I need to correct you on one thing, though. First is the selenium found in grain is selenomethionine, which is more toxic because of its different action/reaction with the body. (more bioavailability).

The problem with too much selenium is more widespread and "under the radar" than the food companies want to believe. Grains are now grown on millions of acres across North and South Dakota, Nebraska, and a few other high selenium states.

We are now figuring out what has been wrong with our swine herd for many years, chronic selenium toxicity that may take years to manifest itself.

Selenium is much more dangerous than vets and food manufacturers have been taught. The feed manufacturing nutritionists have been teaching the vets about nutrition all these years while the company nutritionists have not kept up with the testing of their product for selenium. Ask any food company if they ever test for selenium levels and they will tell you "No". I have already tried with many companies, starting with the largest companies first.

This problem potentially affects all food manufacturing."

Menadione Sodium Bisulfate

While it's a little noticed pet food ingredient, Menadione Sodium Bisulfate (and it's many named variations) is one ingredient to look out for and avoid. This ingredient is commonly found in many dog foods, cat foods, and treats. Unfortunately, it doesn't have the best reputation for being a safe or useful pet food ingredient. Since there are alternatives for pet food makers to use, it makes you wonder why some put our pets at risk.

Menadione Sodium Bisulfate is a synthetic version of vitamin K. You'll see it within the fine print of many pet foods ingredient list. In addition, of course, it's not as simple to find it as it should be. Some pet food ingredient lists will say 'menadione', some with say 'sodium bisulfate', and some will mention vitamin K3 in parenthesis – and these are just a few of the possible variations you have to look for.

This ingredient is added to pet foods and treats as an inexpensive source of vitamin K. In people – deficiencies of vitamin K can lead to blood clotting particularly in the stomach and can lead to intestinal complications. An example for pets, veterinarians will administer an injection of K1 (not the synthetic K3) to a pet who has consumed a rat poison which causes internal bleeding. Food sources of natural vitamin K (K1) are green leafy vegetables; which are not on the 'top ten' list of many pets. Pet food ingredients that could provide natural sources of vitamin K are alfalfa and kelp. However, as you probably have figured out, synthetic vitamin K or menadione is a great deal less expensive than the natural sources of alfalfa and kelp.

Knowing that a pet food company would opt for a synthetic ingredient in contrast to a natural ingredient is bad enough, but it takes one step further on the 'bad scale' with Menadione Sodium Bisulfate. This ingredient can be highly toxic in high doses. Hazard information regarding menadione lists "*carcinogenic effects*" and states "*the substance is toxic to kidneys, lungs, liver, mucous membranes. Repeated or prolonged exposure to the substance can produce target organs damage.*" (63)

With the science based information available on this ingredient, there is no sound reason for menadione to be considered as a pet food or pet treat ingredient; that is other than a big money saver for a pet food company. AAFCO and the FDA have no restrictions to the use of menadione in pet foods, and the pet food can even proudly claim 'Natural' on the label even if it contains this un-natural ingredient. Look at the fine print of your pet's food and treats for menadione; sources of natural vitamin K (alfalfa and kelp) seem to be a far better option.

Heavy Metal Testing of Pet Foods

Spex CertiPrep is a laboratory standards company. Every couple of years they test a product line to bring attention to their company. In 2010 Spex CertiPrep tested pet food; they discovered pet foods contain a lot more than the advertised choice cuts of meat and fresh vegetables. Some pet foods contain toxic levels of arsenic, lead, mercury, and more.

Quoting the Paper "*Analysis of Toxic Trace Metals in Pet Foods Using Cryogenic Grinding and Quantitation by ICP-MS, Part 1*" (64) published in the January 2011 Spectroscopy Magazine...

"*For this investigation 58 cat and dog foods were bought from local stores or donated by the authors and other pet owners. The samples consisted of 31 dry food and 27 wet food varieties. Of the 31 dry foods, 18 were dog food and 13 were cat food samples. The wet foods comprised 13 dog food and 14 cat food samples, representing pet food contained in cans and pouches.*"

"*Pet food prices ranged from the "bargain" store foods priced at $0.02/oz to gourmet or specialty foods purchased from pet suppliers priced at $0.42/oz. Three canned foods for human consumption were tested, including tuna fish, sardines, and chicken, which were sampled for comparison and control purposes.*"

"*The analysis of all the pet food samples showed that the highest concentrations of toxic elements were found in the dry foods of both cats and dogs. Out of the elements studied, dry food had the highest elemental content for 13 of the 15 elements examined. Dog food had the highest result for nine of the 15 toxic elements and cat food had the highest concentration for six of the 15 elements.*"

"*The dry dog food contained the highest concentrations of the following elements: beryllium, cadmium, cesium, antimony, thorium, thallium, uranium, and vanadium. The wet dog foods contained lower concentrations of the toxic elements studied than the dry dog foods. The dry cat foods contained the highest results for five of the 15 elements including arsenic, cobalt, molybdenum, nickel, and lead. The wet cat foods showed the overall lowest concentrations of the toxic elements studied than any of the other pet foods studied.*"

"*The presence of several other elements in some of the pet food samples was unexpected. Uranium, beryllium, and thorium are often associated with nuclear energy and mining. As stated earlier, concentrations of over 500 µg/kg of uranium were found in several of the dry dog food samples. A few of the dry cat food samples had concentrations of over 200 µg/kg of uranium. In these samples of high uranium concentrations, there were also found to be the highest concentrations of both beryllium and thorium.*"

Here are some of the findings from their pet food testing...

As - Arsenic.

Pet Food Average 95 ppb
Pet Food Max 290 ppb
Human Tuna - 14 ppb
Human Sardines - 30 ppb
Human Chicken - 4.4 ppb.

Be - Beryllium.
Pet Food Average 8.6 ppb
Pet Food Max 74 ppb
Human Tuna 6.1 ppb
Human Sardines - 3.7 ppb
Human Chicken - 2.9 ppb

Cd - Cadmium.
Pet Food Average 42 ppb
Pet Food Max 130 ppb
Human Tuna 36 ppb
Human Sardines 14 ppb
Human Chicken 1.8 ppb

Co - Cobalt.
Pet Food Average 200 ppb
Pet Food Max 920 ppb
Human Tuna 23 ppb
Human Sardines 44 ppb
Human Chicken 25 ppb

Cr - Chromium.
Pet Food Average 480 ppb
Pet Food Max 2500 ppb
Human Tuna 25 ppb
Human Sardines 41 ppb
Human Chicken 20 ppb

Cs - Caesium.
Pet Food Average 9.0 ppb
Pet Food Max 28 ppb
Human Tuna 14 ppb
Human Sardines 16 ppb

Human Chicken 2.7 ppb

Hg - Mercury.
Pet Food Average 37 ppb
Pet Food Max 560 ppb
Human Tuna 89 ppb
Human Sardines - ND (non detectable)
Human Chicken - ND

Ms - Molybdenum.
Pet Food Average 550 ppb
Pet Food Max 2300 ppb
Human Tuna 6.2 ppb
Human Sardines 9.3 ppb
Human Chicken 23 ppb

Ni - Nickel.
Pet Food Average 980 ppb
Pet Food Max 3200 ppb
Human Tuna 180 ppb
Human Sardines 380 ppb
Human Chicken 950 ppb

Pb - Lead.
Pet Food Average 210 ppb
Pet Food Max 5900 ppb
Human Tuna 7.2 ppb
Human Sardines 11 ppb
Human Chicken 3.2 ppb

Sb - Antimony.
Pet Food Average 75 ppb
Pet Food Max 970 ppb
Human Tuna 0.90 ppb
Human Sardines 1.6 ppb
Human Chicken 1.2 ppb

Se - Selenium.
Pet Food Average 330 ppb

Pet Food Max 1500 ppb
Human Tuna 360 ppb
Human Sardines 320 ppb
Human Chicken 147 ppb

Sn - Tin.
Pet Food Average 350 ppb
Pet Food Max 9400 ppb
Human Tuna 98 ppb
Human Sardines 28 ppb
Human Chicken 0 5.8 ppb

Th - Thorium.
Pet Food Average 14 ppb
Pet Food Max 87 ppb
Human Tuna - ND
Human Sardines 0.10 ppb
Human Chicken 0.08 ppb

Tl - Thallium.
Pet Food Average 4.0 ppb
Pet Food Max 10 ppb
Human Tuna 1.0 ppb
Human Sardines 3.1 ppb
Human Chicken 1.8 ppb

U - Uranium.
Pet Food Average 91 ppb
Pet Food Max 860 ppb
Human Tuna 0.20 ppb
Human Sardines 6.0 ppb
Human Chicken 0.20 ppb

V - Vanadium.
Pet Food Average 280 ppb
Pet Food Max 7400 ppb
Human Tuna 6.2 ppb
Human Sardines 5.2 ppb
Human Chicken 5.6 ppb

Conclusions published in the abstract...

"Toxic Element Exposure for Cats"

"A 10-lb cat eating 1 cup a day (100 g) of dry food or 1 small can of wet food (175 g) with the maximum contamination would be consuming about:

29 mcg (micrograms) Arsenic (greater than 20 times Reference Dosage limit)

13 mcg Cadmium (greater than 3 times the Reference Dosage limit)

17 mcg Mercury (greater than 30 times the Reference Dosage limit)

42 mcg Uranium (greater than 3 times the Reference Dosage limit)"

"Dry cat food contained more contamination which exceeded human Reference Dosage guidelines than wet cat food."

"Toxic Element Exposure for Dogs"

"A 50-lb dog eating 5 cups (500 g) a day of dry food or 1 large can of wet food (375 g) with the maximum contamination would be consuming about:

124 mcg (micrograms) of Arsenic (greater than 20 times Reference Dosage limit)

65 mcg of Cadmium (greater than 2 times Reference Dosage limit)

280 mcg of Mercury (greater than 120 times Reference Dosage limit)

5 mcg of Thallium (greater than 2 times Reference Dosage limit)

430 mcg Uranium (greater than 5 times Reference Dosage limit)

1200 mcg Vanadium (greater than 6 times Reference Dosage limit)"

"The average dry dog food exceed the Reference Dosage levels for many compounds and wet dog food had fewer results exceeding the human Reference Dosage limits."

"Dry dog food had the largest number of significant toxic metals overall."

"Seven samples of pet food contained significant amounts of Uranium from 500 to 2000 ppb."

As of the publishing of this book, no regulatory authority has commented on these toxic levels of heavy metals discovered in pet foods.

On Feb. 5th he didn't want to eat. Feb. 6th I bought him canned dog food and by the end of the day he ate two cans of it. But realized that by Feb. 7th it was best to take him to the vets especially since he would not eat and he had also developed an occasional cough just a couple weeks prior, as though he was gagging on something.

Not only did the vet take blood and stool samples but also took x-rays of his chest and abdomen. He was showing signs of dehydration so it was best he spend the night. The x-rays showed signs of bronchitis and possible pneumonia. It also appeared that there was water near his heart.

Feb. 9 I picked him up at the vets after another x-ray was taken which showed that there seemed to be an improvement. He still wasn't eating till I took him to the car and he ate his treats. When we got home he refused any dog food but did eat by the end of the day a couple boiled chicken breasts and some rice.

Feb. 11th he would not eat again so I took him back to the vets where an ultrasound was performed. It appeared in the chest area things were improving somewhat, one side of his heart was very strong the other side was strong for a dog 10 years old. This did not surprise me for up till Feb 5th he was still playing with my other dog and wanting to catch his Frisbee and chase after the birds and the squirrels, but now there was a concern with a thickness in his colon. His medicines where changed hoping that it would

101

help clear out his stomach which seemed extremely bloated, he was now having no bowel movement.

Feb. 13th there was no improvement; he was obviously growing weaker, still wanting to drink water which was now causing him to throw up a yellow liquid. I have very good vets who then met me at the clinic and on Feb. 14th it was arranged for me to take him to a specialist.

The specialist began by taking his temperature, which was normal, doing an outer physical examination, looking at the x-rays and results of tests forwarded by my vets. The specialist began to speak about a possible cancer as well as a fungal bacteria, histoplasmosis, and was inclined to believe cancer since histoplasmosis was something found up North and not in our area.

The specialist then took my dog for a more thorough ultrasound, after which he came and laid by my feet as the results were being reviewed. Some-time after the assistant came in saying that we needed to put my dog on the table so that his eyes could be checked. When the specialist came back into the room the first question was, "Where do you live?" "Urban or a rural area?" "Does your dog spend a lot of time outside?" Now there seemed to be a greater concern of a possible bacterial infection and the fact the lining of his colon was so thick. It was difficult to see much into his stomach or the colon because of the stomach being bloated and the thick lining of the colon.

It was then decided that I would go home for the evening and bring my dog back in the morning so that the specialist could get a sample from his lung and go into his colon as far as would be possible.

I drove back home with my dogs, concerned now about the possible fungal bacteria and the cause of this. I began to do some research on what might cause a fungal bacteria, the more I studied about histoplasmosis I realized and was assured by my vets, that this was not the problem. But then I began to look further and reflect on what was the change in his lifestyle that may have lead to a fungal bacteria of any type. I began to read about allergies and the cause of them. The more I read and studied I was lead to sites that spoke about food allergies and problems with different dog foods.

Having two dogs, one being three years older than the other, I always gave them the same food after their puppy years. When I changed to Science Diet I put both of them on, feeding them each the same amount, it was pointed out to me after my dog died that prior to my feeding them Science Diet, my dog who died would never beg for food. He was

102

the one who always barked when my other dog got into food. My other dog was good at always finding something else to eat so not only was my other dog on Science Diet he was also on some healthy table food, unlike my dog who died who only ate the Science Diet.

When I got home with my dogs, I picked my sick dog up out of my car and he was gasping for air, I set his bed up for him by my couch, not wanting him to have to walk up the stairs. That night I thought I'd sleep on the couch with my dog on his bed next to me. He was having difficulty breathing and it was suggested that maybe a vaporizer might help and so I called my vet for advice and was told that a vaporizer or putting him in a steamy bathroom, may help clear the breathing. I chose to go buy a vaporizer. When I returned home I found that my dog walked from his bed to go lay on the rug by the patio door. I took a picture of him laying there as he was looking at me. About ten minutes later he stood up and began to take the long route around the dining room table to his water bowl. He was having some difficulty walking. As he stood in front of his water bowl, he looked over at me and then he collapsed on the floor with his legs spread eagle. He lay there looking at me. I picked him up to lay him back on his bed. As I lay him there, still holding him in my arms, he was gasping for air, made a gurgling sound, he closed his eyes and died.

I drove him to the vet that night, who took a biopsy of him. When the results returned, nothing stated that he had cancer but it was obvious there were some problems in his colon. Since then, I have read a great deal more on bacterial infection in which so many are speaking out about Science Diet pet foods. I am not going to draw any conclusion to any of this for as I have said, I am not a nutritionist nor a vet.

This was my experience. This is my story. This was my dog, my faithful companion.

Nick

Probiotics

Some pet food companies boast about healthy prebiotics and/or probiotics in their foods. Scientific research on the other hand has proven that many of these health claims are no more than fancy marketing tactics; science has shown many pet foods probiotics are not live and viable thus would provide no benefit to the pet. Should pet owners believe the hype of pre- and probiotics? The answer seems to be in the pet food Guaranteed Analysis.

It's no wonder pet owners notice pet foods that tout phrases such as 'promotes healthy digestion'. 'Unhealthy digestion' - you know, things like diarrhea and gas (yikes) can be quite motivational to cure. There is probably not a pet owner on the planet that has not experienced the 'fun' of cleaning a carpet stain from un-healthy digestion problems of a pet. So of course, when a pet owner notices claims that a pet food promotes healthy digestion, the product sale could be influenced on those claims (and the memories of gas and carpet cleaning).

But…how can a pet owner know if these health claims touted on pet food labels are the real deal? There is a way…but first, pet owners need to know what they are buying; a good understanding of pre- and probiotics.

Dr. J. Scott Weese DVM DVSc DipACVIM of Ontario Veterinary College defines prebiotics as "*essentially food for probiotics (and potentially other intestinal bacteria). They are substances that are neither absorbed nor digested by the body and which are used to stimulate the growth of beneficial intestinal microorganisms. Examples of prebiotics are fructooligosaccharides (FOS), inulin and guar gum.*" Dr. Weese quotes numerous other researchers to define probiotics as "*living micro-organisms that, when administered orally in adequate numbers, provide a health benefit to the host beyond that of their inherent nutritional value.*" (65)

In unscientific terms, prebiotics are food for probiotics; probiotics are friendly bacteria that helps to keep the tummy in good working order. Of great importance to pet owners paying high dollar prices for premium ingredient pet food, "*it is a well-established fact that the intestinal micro-flora influence the digestion and absorption of food, the function of the immune system, peristalsis, production of vitamins such as B-vitamins and influence the turnover of the intestinal epithelial cells.*" (66) Considering 80% of the immune system is located in your pets (and your) intestinal system, keeping the 'pipes' in good working order promotes a stronger immune system.

While many pet foods tout marketing claims of prebiotics and probiotics, are they really benefiting your pet?

Science says yes, if the bacteria is live and viable; which brings up another issue of concern with pet food. Todd R. Klaenhammer writes in an abstract of the Southeast Dairy Foods Research Center and Department of Food Science, College of Agriculture and Life Sciences, North Carolina State University "*Over the course of the symposium, evidence was presented to illustrate the following benefits elicited by probiotics, prebiotics and synbiotics: 1) pathogen interference, exclusion and antagonism; 2) immunostimulation and immunomodulation; 3) anticarcinogenic and antimutagenic activities in animal models; 4) alleviation of symptoms of lactose intolerance; 5) vaginal/urinary tract health; 6) reduction in blood pressure in hypertensive subjects; 7) decreased incidence and duration of diarrhea (antibiotic-associated diarrhea, Clostridium difficile, travelers and rotaviral); and 8) mainte-nance of mucosal integrity.*" (67)

Numerous research papers have indicated far more study of pro-biotics and prebiotics is necessary to completely understand the potential benefits (for pets and people). However, what we do know is very encouraging.

Science has also shown that although many pet foods include probiotics in their ingredient listing, many pet foods did not contain live, viable organisms. Of nineteen commercial pet foods tested in one study, twelve contained a probiotic variety (bacterial fermentation products), that were not true live beneficial organisms. Further, no pet foods contained all of the probiotics listed on the label. "*Overall, the actual contents of the diets were not accurately represented by the label descriptions.*" (68)

Another study scrutinized 44 human or veterinary probiotics. "*Organisms were improperly identified in 43% human and 35% veterinary products.*" In only 2 veterinary products were the contents of the probiotic "*adequately identified.*" (69)

This is discouraging science for pet owners that believe in the benefits of probiotics. However, there are some pet food manufacturers that are proving to pet owners their probiotics are live and viable; you'll find it in the Guaranteed Analysis.

The Guaranteed Analysis of a pet food label is required by regulation to provide pet owners with 'guaranteed' nutrient levels of the pet food. No pet food company, that includes probiotics in their formula, is required by regulation to include probiotic guarantees in the Guaranteed Analysis on the label. Yet some do. We can only assume that those small handful of pet food companies that include a 'guaranteed' statement of propbiotic levels on their label and/or on their website is telling us…they guarantee the probiotic to be live and viable. We can as well assume that the pet food companies that include probiotics in their ingredient list (and marketing) yet exclude probiotic guarantees on their label or website is probably not live and viable (perhaps one of the pet foods studied in the research above).

Yes, any pet food company can state all types of percentages within a Guaranteed Analysis and few (if any) would ever get caught lying to petsumers. However, in a rapidly changing pet food world, I believe a clear show of guarantees listed on a pet food label and/or website is our best bet at holding them accountable for their claims. Don't pay any attention to slick marketing tag lines, look at the ingredients AND the guaranteed analysis (look both on the label and on the pet food website). Educated pet owners know pet food can 'talk the talk'; we're looking for those that can 'walk the walk' to feed to our pets. Guarantees are part of 'the walk'.

Omegas

Three studies show that dogs fed fish oil (high omega-3 fatty acid) improved in mobility and showed less pain. Believers of the power of fish oil (myself included) are not surprised, but at least now we have clinical proof.

The American Veterinary Medical Association (AVMA) announced in a press release the results of the three studies. The studies included 274 dogs with osteoarthritis that participated at dozens of private veterinary clinics and two University veterinary clinics.

"In the first study, dogs with chronic pain associated with osteoarthritis showed improvements in their ability to play and rise from rest at six weeks after being switched to a diet containing high concentrations of fish oil omega-3 fatty acids. The second study showed that limb strength in dogs improved with omega-3 dietary intervention. In the third study, veterinarians were able to reduce the dosage of carprofen, a common NSAID used for pain relief in dogs with osteoarthritis, while still providing pain relief to dogs that were fed food supplemented with omega-3 fatty acids." (70)

Study One was published in the Journal of the American Veterinary Medical Association (JAVMA) January 1, 2010. In this study 38 client owned dogs with osteoarthritis were examined at 2 University veterinary clinics. *"Dogs were randomly assigned to receive a typical commercial food (n = 16) or a test food (22) containing 3.5% fish oil omega-3 fatty acids. On day 0 (before the trial began) and days 45 and 90 after the trial began, investigators conducted orthopedic evaluations and force-plate analyses of the most severely affected limb of each dog, and owners completed questionnaires to characterize their dogs' arthritis signs."* Conclusions and Clinical Relevance: *"At least in the short term, dietary supplementation with fish oil omega-3 fatty acids resulted in an improvement in weight bearing in dogs with osteoarthritis."* (71)

Study Two did things a bit differently; they used high doses of fish oil. Published in the JAVMA on January 1, 2010. In this study 127 client owned dogs with osteoarthritis in 1 or more joints were examined from 18 private veterinary clinics. *"Dogs were randomly assigned to be fed for 6 months with a typical commercial food or a test food containing a 31-fold increase in total omega-3 fatty acid content and a 34-fold decrease in omega-6–omega-3 ratio, compared with the control food. Dog owners completed a questionnaire about their dog's arthritic condition, and investigators performed a physical examination and collected samples for a CBC and serum biochemical analyses (including measurement of fatty acids concentration) at the onset of the study and at 6, 12, and 24 weeks afterward."* Results: *"According to owners, dogs fed the test food had a significantly improved ability to rise from a resting position and play at 6 weeks and improved ability to walk at 12 and 24 weeks, compared with control dogs."* (72)

Study Three was to determine if pain medicine could be reduced by supplementing the pet's diet with fish oil omega-3 fatty acids. Published in the JAVMA on March 1, 2010, 101 client owned dogs with stable chronic osteoarthritis were examined at 33 privately owned veterinary hospitals. *"In all dogs, the dosage of carprofen was standardized over a 3-week period to approximately 4.4 mg/kg/d (2 mg/lb/d), PO. Dogs were then randomly assigned to receive a food supplemented with fish oil omega-3 fatty acids or a control food with low omega-3 fatty acid content, and 3, 6, 9, and 12 weeks later, investigators made decisions regarding increasing or decreasing the carprofen dosage on the basis of investigator assessments of 5 clinical signs and owner assessments of 15 signs."* Results: *"Results suggested that in dogs with chronic osteoarthritis receiving carprofen because of signs of pain, feeding a diet supplemented with fish oil omega-3 fatty acids may allow for a reduction in carprofen dosage."* (73)

Of huge importance is the following statement in the AVMA release: *"This finding is especially important because it allows veterinarians to better understand that complications that may arise from pain relief medications could be reduced when the medications are used in combination with proper nutrition."* We can assume that *"proper nutrition"* in this case implies a diet supplemented with fish oil.

Although none of these studies stated the type or grade of fish oil used, most experts recommended supplementing your pet's diet with a pure pharmaceutical grade fish oil. Inferior fish oils can be contaminated with mercury and other toxins. Always consult your veterinarian regarding any supplements added to their diet.

Warehousing Concerns

The following was a press release distributed by the FDA on June 19, 2008...

FDA Requests Seizure of Animal Food Products at PETCO Distribution Center

Today (June 19, 2008), at the request of the U.S. Food and Drug Administration (FDA), U.S. Marshals seized various animal food products stored under unsanitary conditions at the PETCO Animal Supplies Distribution Center located in Joliet, Ill., pursuant to a warrant issued by the United States District Court in Chicago.

U.S. Marshals seized all FDA-regulated animal food susceptible to rodent and pest contamination. The seized products violate the Federal Food, Drug, and Cosmetic Act because it was alleged in a case filed by the United States Attorney that they were being held under unsanitary conditions. (The Act uses the term "insanitary" to describe such conditions).

During an FDA inspection of a PETCO distribution center in April, widespread and active rodent and bird infestation was found. The FDA inspected the facility again in May and found continuing and widespread infestation.

"We simply will not allow a company to store foods under filthy and unsanitary conditions that occur as a direct result of the company's failure to adequately control and prevent pests in its facility," said Margaret O'K. Glavin, Associate Commissioner for Regulatory Affairs. "Consumers expect that such safeguards will be in place not only for human food, but for pet food as well."

The distribution center in Joliet, Ill., provides pet food products and supplies to PETCO retail stores in 16 states including Alabama, Illinois, Indiana, Iowa, Kansas, Kentucky, Louisiana, Michigan, Minnesota, Missouri, Nebraska, Ohio, Oklahoma, Tennessee, Texas, and Wisconsin.

FDA has no reports of pet illness or death associated with consumption of animal food distributed by PETCO, and does not have evidence that the food is unsafe for animals. However, the seized products were in permeable packages and held under conditions that could affect the food's integrity and quality.

As a precaution, consumers who have handled products originating from the PETCO distribution center should thoroughly wash their hands with hot water and soap. Any surfaces that came in contact with the packages should be washed as well. Consumers are further advised as a precaution to thoroughly wash products sold in cans and glass containers from PETCO in the 16 affected states.

If a pet has become ill after eating these food products, pet owners should contact their veterinarian and report illnesses to FDA state consumer complaint coordinators. (75)

While a pet food manufacturer might use the highest quality of ingredients and search high and low for the most trusted suppliers, improper pet food warehousing could contaminate the food.

With every purchase of a pet food or treat, make sure the bag is not torn or stained. Make sure the can is not dented or swollen. Once you open the bag or can, closely examine the food. Does it look and smell as it did the last time? If it in any way, looks or smells different, return it to the pet food store. Don't risk your pet's health.

Pet Food Personal Experience - Sophie

My Airedale, Sophie, was 12 years old and I always fed premium canned food to her (and our toy Poodle, Pearl). I live outside of Wheatland, WY and thus would get my dog food from Fort Collins, a 2 hour drive one way. I usually fed Canidae or Wellness canned, sometimes Natural Balance. I was already a label reader since Sophie had skin problems. I ran out of canned food and a friend recommended Safeway canned to tide me over till I could get to Ft Collins. Her dogs all ate it now and then. So I picked up 6 cans of their brand.

My toy Poodle, Pearl, refused to eat any of it, which was interesting because she loves canned food. Anyhow, Sophie ate all 6 cans. Within a few days she had acute kidney failure. She had already been diagnosed with a heart murmur a couple years past. I thought she had had a stroke, and took her into the vet when she collapsed. She was then diagnosed and was pretty much shut down, depressed, tired out. I know my vet thought I would be back within a few days to have her put to sleep. My vet bill was only $180 for blood and urine workups. Not much could be done according to my vet.

At that time I had no clue about the melamine. So, I proceeded to look up kidney diets and made homemade food for her and she recovered mentally, but had to wear diapers. I kept her with me and happy for 3 more months until the combination of heart

113

and kidney problems forced me to let her go. It was one day at a time for weeks, but as long as she had quality of life, a happy outlook, I held on to her. She was a very independent and hard headed dog, typical of many female Airedales, and she was my heart dog.

She woke me up on her last nite with fluid in her lungs and inability to breathe without being propped up, I sat with her and said my goodbyes (she hated cuddling except on her terms) and called the vet. Since they couldn't come out for a few hours, I opted to take Sophie in to their office. I let her go to the rainbow bridge. I felt like most do when they lose their furkids, like I had concrete overshoes on for weeks. I couldn't look at her pictures for months, and still miss her today, and always will. She has been gone since May of 2009.

I have become a rabid label reader, and cook for my dogs now or feed canned and dry that is rated as premium ingredients. I am disgusted with the pet food industry that is more interested in greed and profit than quality in so many instances. I appreciate the companies that do try to make a premium diet and know there are those of us that are label readers, but it is still hard to trust any company.

Deb J.

Pet Food Can Lie

You come home from work and notice your dog or cat peeking at you from around the corner. You immediately know something's up. Regardless of whether you discover a "*present*" left on the living room rug or a broken vase from the cabinet they aren't supposed to be up on, pets can't lie. They tell us the truth every single time. Pet food manufacturers, on the other hand, can lie and keep a straight face every single time.

Changing the name to protect the pet food identity, here is part of the new advertising for a pet food:

"*Healthy Living…Yes, living healthy can be delicious*".

And from the website of the same food (changing some of the wording):
"*Healthy Living Pet Food provides an abundance of tasty, wholesome ingredients giving your pet the perfect balance of nutrition and taste. Your pet will relish the new flavors. The same quality nutrition you enjoy can do the same thing for your pet.*"

Now, here is the actual ingredient list from the pet food that advertises that it's healthy, has an abundance of wholesome ingredients, and implies it's the "*same quality*" as your food:

Ingredients: **chicken by-product meal**, corn gluten meal, ground yellow corn, soybean meal, ground wheat, **animal fat** preserved with mixed-tocopherols (form of Vitamin E), salmon meal, salmon, chicken, powdered cellulose, brewers rice, animal liver flavor, soybean hulls, malt extract, phosphoric acid, calcium carbonate, salt, choline chloride, dried spinach, parsley flakes, dried cranberries, dried carrots, dried cheese powder, potassium chloride, taurine, **added color (Red 40, Yellow 6, Yellow 5, Blue 2)**, Vitamin E supplement, zinc sulfate, ferrous sulfate, manganese sulfate, niacin, Vitamin A supplement, calcium pantothenate, thiamine mononitrate, copper sulfate, riboflavin supplement, Vitamin B-12 supplement, pyridoxine hydrochloride, folic acid, Vitamin D-3 supplement, calcium iodate, biotin, **menadione sodium bisulfite** complex (source of Vitamin K activity), sodium selenite.

Every ingredient that is considered risky by many pet food experts was listed in **bold**. 'By-products' and any variation such as "*chicken by-product meal*" in this pet food are leftover ingredients from the processing of human foods, bits and pieces of meat-producing animals that are NOT considered safe or desirable as "*people food*". These bits and pieces can also come from drugged or diseased animals rejected for use in human food. "*Animal fat*" is the pet food ingredient the FDA determined to be most likely to contain a euthanized animal and the drug used to euthanize it. "*Added color*" is added to some pet foods to make it look more appealing to the pet owner. Color provides no nutritional value to the pet. "*Menadione sodium bisulfite complex*" is a very controversial synthetic Vitamin K. Does this pet food seem "*healthy*", have an "*abundance of wholesome ingredients*", or look like it's "*the same quality nutrition you enjoy*"? I don't think so either.

Even though few pet owners would agree that the advertising tactics of this pet food company and many others is fair and honest, the rules of pet food manufacturing allow this. "*Unqualified claims, either directly or indirectly*" are legally acceptable within existing regulations.

So let me ask you a question. If you were driving on the German autobahn where the recommended driving speed is 81 miles per hour but there is no speed limit, would you drive 81 miles per hour even if other cars are zooming past you? Very few would! Very few do!

Now that I've got you thinking, why should a pet food manufacturer tell you their pet food contains "*an abundance of leftover bits and pieces rejected for use in human food*" when they don't have to?

Don't misinterpret my point. I STILL think it's wrong. However, until pet food regulations change and every pet food producer must provide accurate and honest information on its labels and in its advertising, why should pet food manufacturers drive the recommended speed when there is no speed limit?

Pet Food Partial Truths

A concerned pet owner emailed her pet food company asking about the fish meal ingredient. *"Does the fish meal contain ethoxyquin?"* This was the reply she received:

"As a pet food manufacturer XXX maintains an uncompromising position of integrity, honesty and transparency when it comes to the quality of our products and our message to customers and pet parents. Unfortunately in today's pet industry, there are so many myths and misconceptions related to pet nutrition, ingredients and manufacturing practices that we find it important to help you better understand the subject. At XXX we are always about transparency and openness, offering factual information about our products. There has long been speculation and often misinformation relative to preservatives in pet foods. Much of this comes from internet blogs and chat rooms. The information is generally opinion without factual support.

At XXX we strive to procure only the highest quality ingredients that are 100% natural and free from chemical preservatives. All XXX products when produced are always naturally preserved utilizing Naturox as an antioxidant. Naturox, a registered trademark, is an all natural, free flowing antioxidant for use in the preservation of oils, fats, fat-soluble vitamins, flavors, aromas, carotenoids and other oxygen-sensitive material. Ethoxyquin is never used as an antioxidant during our manufacturing process, and we continually test other brands of pet food to make sure we are below tested levels or within standards of our category.

All XXX products meet or exceed AAFCO (Association of American Feed Control Officials) nutrient profiles and are manufactured in USDA-approved facilities with consistently superior Good Manufacturing and Food Safety Audits scores of 95% or above. XXX is committed to providing the highest standard of excellence for nutritional benefit, palatability, product safety, and customer satisfaction. We understand the level of trust that our customers have come to expect from us and from our products. It is our responsibility and commitment to continue to deliver on that trust!"

Did you catch the partial truth?

After three paragraphs of self-proclaiming wonderment (similar to the responses you receive from your Representatives in Congress), this pet food company says *"All XXX products when produced are always naturally preserved utilizing Naturox...*" The partial truth comes from the words "*when produced*".

Pet food regulations do not require a pet food company to list ingredients on labels that they, the manufacturer, did not add. So...fish meal could be and often is preserved with ethoxyquin by the fish meal supplier and the pet owner would be none the wiser by looking at the ingredient panel on the pet food. The pet food manufacturer didn't add the preservative, the ingredient supplier did, so the pet food manufacturer is off the hook to list ethoxyquin.. "*We didn't add it so all is well!*"

This pet food company goes on to say, "*Ethoxyquin is never used as an antioxidant during our manufacturing process,...*" Partial truth..."*during our manufacturing process.*"

The truth is that this particular pet food company recently changed to a fish meal supplier using Naturox instead of ethoxyquin. Prior to this recent change, they did indeed use a non-natural, risky chemical preservative in their pet foods, ethoxyquin, by way of the ingredient fish meal. Their email goes on and on about honesty and transparency and blames blogs and chat rooms for misinformation when actually they themselves are the biggest provider of misinformation.

The truth is that all **XXX** products have not always been preserved using natural methods as their partial truth response claims. It doesn't matter if "*when produced*" or "*during manufacturing*" the company did not add a risky chemical. What matters is that the pets consuming this food were still consuming a risky chemical.

It should NOT be the responsibility of the pet owner to do detective work in order to learn about ingredients in a pet food. But it is.

More Partial Truths

We've all heard the horror stories of what's really in by-products. TruthaboutPetFood.com and our team of secret pet food shoppers decided to see what pet food companies would say about what's really in these ingredients. What they told us is not surprising.

Here are the questions from our secret pet food shoppers sent to various pet food companies that use by-products and/or the ingredient animal fat in their foods/treats:

"I've been reading some concerning things about by-products. Because I feed my pets your XXX and you have the by-product "chicken by-product meal" (or animal fat) listed in the ingredients, I'd like to know EXACTLY what animals and/or animal parts are included in this ingredient. Where do you purchase these by-products? Do any of the animal parts in the by-products come from animals that have died (not been slaughtered) or been euthanized? Does your supplier use any denaturing agents on these animals or animal parts? If yes, what type of denaturing product is used? Finally, what type of preservative is used by your supplier for the by-products?"

Now, here are the responses we received:

Eukanuba/Iams
"I hope your dogs are doing well on Eukanuba Sensitive Stomach. I will be happy to address your concern about chicken by-product meal.

Chicken by-product meal may include stuff that people have a cultural aversion to eating but that doesn't make it a bad source of protein. It is an excellent and complete source of protein because it provides each of the amino acids that are essential to good nutrition for dogs and cats.

Not every chicken by-product meal is as good as ours. Our chicken by-product meal is muscle and internal organs (including intestines) that have been cleaned, dried, cooked, and ground. By industry definition, chicken by-product meal can contain the feet of the chicken - but that's not an acceptable source of protein for us, so our suppliers make every effort to keep the feet out of our chicken by-product meal.

In addition to the superior quality specifications we set for our suppliers, we take additional steps to ensure our chicken by-product meal is the best. We put it through a proprietary screening process to further improve its protein quality. This quality assurance process costs more, but it's part of what makes our chicken by-product meal different.

If you look at how wolves and lions eat in the wild, one of the first things they eat after they've killed their supper is the underbelly of the animal. We may think it's gross to eat intestines, but these ancestors of the dog and cat relish that part of their dinner.

Would you like to read more about our chicken? We have additional information available at our web site. Simply copy-and-paste the following URL to your web browser: http://us.iams.com/iams/en_US/jsp/IAMS_Page.jsp? pageID=A&articleID=261

If you have additional questions, please contact us anytime through our E-mail Us Now page located on our web site at www.Eukanuba.com. Or, look for instant answers on our web site FAQ. We would also welcome your call Monday through Friday from 9:00 a.m. to 7:00 p.m. Eastern Time at 800-423-6036

Thank you for choosing Eukanuba!

Sincerely,
Sharon
Eukanuba Breed Expert"

Eukanuba did not answer all questions. They did not respond to the question of slaughtered or dead/euthanized animals. They did not respond to the question of denaturing agent. They did not respond to the question of preservative used. They did not respond to the *"where ingredients are purchased"* question.

Iams response to these questions was exactly the same as Eukanuba's.

Cesar Canine Cuisine
"In response to your email.

Thank you for taking the time to contact us regarding your experience with our products.

We pride ourselves on the quality of our products and would like the opportunity to discuss this matter in more detail. Please give us a call at 1-800-525-5273, Monday through Friday, between the hours of 8:00 a.m. and 4:30 p.m. Central Standard time. When calling, please refer to this file reference number: 010887731A.

Your confidence in our products and continued goodwill are very important to us."

Cesar Canine Cuisine did not answer any questions.

Diamond Pet Food

"Thank you for your inquiry. Chicken by-product meal is made only from chickens. It is made primarily from the internal organs of the chickens, but there may also be some heads and necks included. It is made from the parts of the chicken that are not used for other purposes. The birds are slaughtered, not dead already (and not euthanized). There are not any denaturing agents used and the ingredient is preserved only with mixed-tocopherols (Vitamin E)."

Diamond Pet Food gave an almost complete answer. They did not respond to the *"where ingredients are purchased"* question.

Purina Pet Food

"Thank you for contacting Nestlé Purina PetCare Company.

We appreciate your interest in our products. Purina(r) Dog Chow(r) brand Dog Food - Healthy Life Nutrition(tm) Complete & Balanced contains poultry by-product meal. Poultry by-product meal consists of chicken (and can include turkey) meat which contains ground, rendered, clean parts of the carcass of slaughtered poultry and some of the internal organs (i.e.: liver and undeveloped eggs), which is then ground and partially dried. It does not contain feathers except in trace amounts as may unavoidably occur even with good factory practice. It is used in pet foods to provide a rich source of protein, fat and minerals.

Its contribution/benefit: rich source of protein, fat and minerals. Its source: chicken and/or turkey.

Dog Chow also contains animal fat preserved with mixed-tocopherols (a form of Vitamin E, used as a preservative).

Over 30 years ago, the FDA (Food & Drug Administration) approved the use of ethoxyquin in human and animal foods. Prior to its approval by the FDA, ethoxyquin underwent several years of intensive efficacy and safety studies.

Ethoxyquin is an antioxidant used in some of our pet foods to prevent fat from becoming rancid. Rancidity not only produces an unpleasant odor, it can also destroy fat-soluble vitamins in the diet.

Over the years, pet foods using ethoxyquin as a preservative have been fed to countless dogs and cats. Hundreds of feeding studies by reputable pet food manufacturers using the appropriate levels of ethoxyquin as a preservative have not revealed any health problems caused by its use.

A refined version of ethoxyquin has some use in human foods. It preserves color in chili powder and paprika. The EPA (Environmental Protection Agency) has approved its use on apples and pears to keep bruises from oxidizing and turning brown after the food is picked.

We hope this information is helpful and that you will let us know if you have any other questions.

Again, thank you for visiting our web site."

Purina did respond to type of animals used in by-products but did not respond to types of animals used in the ingredient animal fat. They responded to the slaughtered or non-slaughtered animals question with by-products but again did not respond to the same question regarding animal fat. They did not respond to the use of denaturing agent. They did not respond to the "*where ingredients are purchased*" question.

Rachael Ray's Nutrish Pet Food
"Thank you for contacting us with your questions. I assure you that we do not use any euthanized pets or any other sort of 'dead' animals. The 'fat' in each formula is from what that formula is. In other words... the fat in the Chicken & Veggie formula is from chicken, and the fat in the Beef & Brown Rice formula is from beef. And our foods are naturally preserved with mixed-tocopherols (Vitamin E).

All of our ingredients are gotten locally within a 100 mile radius of Meadville, P.A.

Should you have any other questions, please feel free to contact me again.

Sincerely,

*Melanie
Ainsworth Pet*

Rachael Ray Nutrish"

Nutrish Pet Food did respond to the slaughtered or non-slaughtered animal question. Nutrish gave a confusing response to the animal fat question. Animal fat by official definition can be from any animal source or a combination of numerous animal sources. As implied by the Nutrish response, if the fat were from chicken, it would be listed as "*chicken fat*" on the label. Nutrish did not respond to the denaturing agent question nor did they respond to the specific animal parts question. Nutrish did provide a partial response to the "*where ingredients are purchased*" question.

Hill's Science Diet

"*Thank you for visiting HillsPet.com and contacting us with your question. Your interest in our Company and our fine products is greatly appreciated.*

The animal fat used in our product comes from pork or chicken, depending on the product. It is in there because it provides essential fatty acids for good skin and shiny hair/coat. It provides proper energy levels and is necessary to maintain health and life itself.

We maintain the highest standards of quality control for our manufacturing facilities, our ingredients, and our finished products. We source meat and poultry ingredients from plants that process foods for human consumption. We utilize rendered poultry by-products which are derived exclusively from chicken and turkey, and rendered lamb meal imported from New Zealand. We require certification and signed affidavits from all our suppliers that they do not include euthanized pets in our raw materials. As part of a vigorous vendor certification program, vendors must test raw ingredients before shipment to our manufacturing facilities.

We appreciate that you took the time to contact us. If you have any further questions or comments, please feel free to call our Consumer Affairs Department toll free at 1-800-445-5777 or visit our website at HillsPet.com.

Consumer Affairs
Hill's Pet Nutrition, Inc."

Science Diet did not respond to the slaughtered or non-slaughtered question. They did not respond to specific animal parts question. They did not respond to the denaturing agent question. They did not respond to the preservative question. They did not respond to the "*where ingredients are purchased*" question.

Pedigree Pet Food
"*In response to your email.*

Thank you for taking the time to contact us regarding your experience with our products.

We pride ourselves on the quality of our products and would like the opportunity to discuss this matter in more detail. Please give us a call at 1-800-525-5273, Monday through Friday, between the hours of 8:00 a.m. and 4:30 p.m. Central Standard time. When calling, please refer to this file reference number: 010887736A.

Your confidence in our products and continued goodwill are very important to us.

David
Mars Petcare US, Inc.
Consumer Response Team
1-800-525-5273"

Pedigree did not respond to any questions.

Just because pet food companies don't give us complete and accurate answers doesn't mean we don't deserve to know. We do! Keep asking those questions. Keep demanding answers.

More from Secret Pet Food Shoppers...
Nona is a cat lover extremely concerned with BPA linings in canned cat food. She wrote Evangers Pet Foods...
"*I subscribe to Petsumer Reports online and they are reporting that your cans contain a BPA lining. Is this true? Veterinary researchers have found a link between BPA in cat food cans and hyper-thyroidism in cats and BPA is regulated by the European Union. I would love to purchase some of your products, but I don't feed any dry food to my cats and I won't purchase any canned food that is contaminated by BPA.*

Thank you.
Nona W"

The next day Nona received the following response from Evangers Pet Food:

"Greetings Nona,

Evanger's contacted our can supplier who assured us that our cans are indeed BPA free.

I hope this helps you during your search for a quality canned food for your cats.

All the best,

-Chelsea Sher"

That's when Nona emailed me asking if what Evangers was telling her was true and perhaps Petsumer wasn't aware of the BPA-free cans used by Evangers. So I called them. This was our conversation:

Me: Do your canned pet foods contain a BPA lining?

Evangers: No.

Me: Are you sure? I thought only the small cans of pet food are available without a BPA lining.

Evangers: Uh, yes.

Me: So, your smaller cans are BPA-free but your larger cans do indeed have a BPA lining. Is this correct?

Evangers: Uh, yes.

When I emailed Nona about my conversation with Evangers, she was more than a little perplexed at the conflicting answers. So, she wrote them again...

"A friend of mine called Evangers and someone at your company admitted that some of Evangers cans are lined with BPA. If Evangers is being dishonest in your responses regarding this question, I certainly won't be able to trust the other ingredients in

your pet food. Which of your cans contain BPA (aka BADGE, Bisphenol-A) and which don't? Will someone please be honest?

Nona W"

And here was their response...

"Greetings Nona,

Until recently the cans that were BPA-free were our 5.5 and 6 oz cans. However, we recently switched our 13 oz cans to a BPA-free can as well. Therefore, your friend may have spoken with us before or during the time of our transition, in which case he or she received accurate information.

We certainly hope this answers your questions. Please feel free to contact me again if you have any other questions.

Regards,

-Chelsea Sher"

So, what's going on here? Is this customer service rep at Evangers hopelessly confused?

Another phone call (from me) to Evangers went as follows:

Me: Do your canned foods contain a BPA lining?

Evangers: Only the small cans. The 5 ounce and 6 ounce cans are BPA-free. There are no options for pet food companies with the large cans. We can't find BPA-free cans. The large cans do have the lowest amount of BPA possible.

Unlike previous replies, this was an honest and clear answer.

Pet Food Personal Experience - Gracie

My 12 year old Shih Tzu "Gracie" started having seizures. The first seizure was almost unnoticeable and I probably wouldn't have seen it except that I had had a miniature Schnauzer with an enlarged heart that had seizures when he got excited. Gracie's second seizure was horrific. She fell over, her back bowed backwards to the point that I thought she was in danger of breaking her spine and she cried out the entire time the seizure lasted, which was at least 30 seconds. It took her about 30 minutes to recover from the seizure once it stopped. I was absolutely helpless to do anything to help her. All I could do was wait for the seizure to end. This happened just before bedtime.

The next day, I went searching online for information about seizures in dogs. I found that Shih Tzu's have no history of seizures and are not prone to have them. I also found an article by a dog owner, about how a lack of nutrition in dog food could cause seizures in dogs. Approximately 2 months passed without another seizure, but then it happened again. By this time, I had read the horror stories about pet food on TruthaboutPetFood.com and remembered the article about the lack of nutrition as a possible cause of seizures in dogs so I bought an expensive brand of both dry and can dog food for Gracie. That was six months ago and Gracie (AKA "Too Cute") hasn't had a seizure since.

Stephen L.

Pet Food Advertising

The Friskies Cat Food commercial currently running on television features a cat dreaming of his perfect food. The tag line of the commercial is *"feed the senses"*. It's puzzling, however, why any cat would dream about purple plastic turkeys, green plastic crabs, and red plastic cows as depicted in the commercial. It's clear what the Friskies Cat Food commercial is trying to imply, that Friskies Cat Food stimulates a cat's senses. What's not clear is why any cat would be stimulated by plastic colored turkeys, fish, cows, and crabs. When you watch the commercial, the cat is *"real"*, the grass and water are *"real"* but all of the implied cat food ingredients are plastic and *"not real"*. What was Friskies thinking?

If cats really do visualize purple plastic turkeys and red plastic cows, perhaps it's because they are eating too much pentobarbital and the euthanized animals that the drug killed. Perhaps one day the FDA will realize that pets consuming a lethal drug in their food turns them into creatures similar to crack cocaine-addicted people, hallucinating cats and dogs dreaming of purple plastic turkeys and red plastic cows. No pet food should be allowed to contain any euthanized animal. No pet food should be a dumping ground for waste.

By the way, federal law prohibits ANY food whether animal or human to contain a diseased animal or an animal that has died any way other than by slaughter. Do pet foods that contain *"meat and bone meal, beef and bone meal, animal fat, and animal digest"* violate federal law? Technically, yes. However, thanks to our friends at the FDA, a *"policy"* has been provided to pet food manufacturers to allow it. FDA policy does not override federal law, but no one seems to care.

If you notice your cat or dog dreaming of purple plastic turkeys, red plastic cows, and green plastic crabs, please check the ingredient list of his/her food. Rehab is only a few steps away in a pet food containing real meat of the same grade/quality you'd give any other member of your family. Intervention is in your hands.

A New York Times article published about Friskies new cat food commercial, the commercial that seems to show the cat hallucinating, gives us some interesting insight on just how much money is spent by the mega pet food manufacturers on advertising. So…with just this one brand of pet food, Friskies, take a guess at how much money is spent on advertising.

"Nestle Purina PetCare spent $17.7 million to advertise the various varieties of Friskies in major media in 2007."

"And increased that to almost $25.9 million in 2008."

"In the first three quarters of 2009, close to $29.7 million was pent to advertise Friskies in major media." (76)

That's a grand total of $73.3 million dollars in less than three years ONLY on advertising in major media for one product.

Who is Chef Michael?

My email to Purina asked the question, *"Who is Chef Michael?"* Below is Purina's response.

"Thank you for contacting Nestlé Purina PetCare Company. We appreciate your interest in our products. Please know that Chef Michael is not a real person but a reflection of the many people inspired to make mealtime special for their dogs.

Purina(r) Chef Michael's(tm) canine creations are a full line of thoughtfully prepared meals designed to give your dog just what he/she desires. Our healthy dry dinners give dogs daily nutrition and extraordinary taste in a blend of tender, meaty pieces and crunchy little bites with vegetable garnishes and other ingredients. Our menu of mouthwatering wet meals is sure to please with the flavors your dog loves and thoughtful touches, like delicious vegetable garnishes.

Because we value you as a loyal consumer, we will be mailing several high value discount coupons for your use toward your next Nestle Purina PetCare Company purchase. Please allow 7-10 business days for delivery.

Again, thank you for visiting our web site."

Turns out that Chef Michael is no one, just pet food marketing.

The Trust of the Innocent Pet Owner

"The trust of the innocent is the liar's most useful tool."
Steven King

Many pet owners, perhaps the greatest majority, walk into any pet store or retail outlet and completely believe every pet food and pet treat label they see. The mere thought that this label might not be 100% honest does not even enter their minds. Why is that?

Your second cousin calls, wanting you to invest money because he's invented a better mouse trap. You don't believe him. You see a television commercial that claims this astounding product will make you look and feel 20 years younger. You don't believe it. However, the majority of pet owners believe pet food television commercials and pet food labels without question. Is it the pictures of innocent dogs and cats? Is it because the bag or can "looks good"?

Regardless of what "*it*" is, "*it*" continues to happen with millions of pet owners unknowingly purchasing dog food, cat food, and pet treats whose ingredients don't quite match television and label claims. For those innocent pet owners being led down the advertising path, here is some truth about pet food regulations, advertising, and labels.

AAFCO, the American Association of Feed Control Officials, develops the pet food regulations on which every U.S. state's pet food regulations are based. Most states accept AAFCO's regulations flatly without change. The FDA, which is responsible for pet food quality and safety, accepts AAFCO's regulations without question. Regulation PF7 of the AAFCO manual, category Nutritional Adequacy, states: *"(a) The label of a pet food or specialty pet food which is intended for all life stages of the pet or specialty pet may include an unqualified claim, directly or indirectly, such as 'complete and balanced', 'perfect', 'scientific' or '100% nutritious'..."*

In other words, pet food manufacturers are allowed to make health claims on pet food labels that are NOT substantiated, not honest, which provide legal permission for the pet food label to lie to you.

Television commercials and pet food labels imply that the pet food contains choice cuts of meat with pictures of such on the label and in the commercial. Some others boldly state that this pet food is the "best" nutrition for your dog or cat. However, what is actually inside the bag or can might be something quite different, something an innocent pet owner would never consider feeding their pet. The common pet food ingredients "*animal fat*" and "*meat and bone meal*" were determined by the FDA to be most likely to contain an animal euthanized because of disease or illness. This means millions of dogs and cats that consume dog foods and cat foods containing these and/or a few other ingredients are likely to be eating not only a diseased animal but also the drug used to end the life of that animal as well. Furthermore, these same pet foods that contain euthanized, diseased animals all make claims of "*Healthy*", "*Premium*", "*Nutritious*", and more.

A lethal drug and a diseased animal don't sound "*nutritious*" to you, do they?

On the flip side, there are many high-quality dog foods, cat foods, and pet treats on the market. However, these companies are forced by pet food regulations to make their labels look exactly like the pet foods that use rendered, euthanized, diseased animals. Unknowing, innocent pet owners strolling down a pet food aisle are defenseless without taking a closer look at the pet food label, specifically the ingredient list.

The pet food/pet treat ingredients that could contain a euthanized, diseased animal are animal fat, meat and bone meal, meat meal, animal digest, and by-product meal. Encourage every pet owner you know to stop being innocent, to stop blindly believing what multi-million dollar advertising is selling them.

Consumer Reports

The March 2009 Consumer Reports told pet owners, "*PRICEY PET FOOD NOT NECESSARILY BETTER*". Don't buy what they are selling you. The inaccurate and misleading Consumer Reports story seems to be merely a marketing piece supporting low-quality pet food manufacturers instead of protecting consumers. Consumer Reports has been a publication that many have depended on for years. The March 2009 edition clearly shows that they didn't do their homework. This misleading article is nothing more than a feature length pet food advertising strategy supporting many untruths about pet food quality and, sadly, directing petsumers to look for the wrong things when choosing a dog food or cat food.

The second paragraph of the Consumer Reports pet food article sets the misleading stage, scaring pet owners with untruthful cost per serving information. The article states that low end pet foods of the WalMart variety would cost a pet owner of a 35 pound dog .38 cents per day versus $2.88 per day for an organic brand. Even more startling (and even more misleading!), is their quoted cost per day for the feeding of canned foods, from $1.38 per day for another WalMart food to $4.78 per day for a higher quality dog food. The truth is far from what Consumer Reports is trying to sell.

When you crunch the numbers and compare the cost per serving of what appears to be cheap pet food versus what appears to be expensive, unaffordable pet food, you'll discover that the difference in cost per serving per day is only pennies. In many cases, higher quality, seemingly higher priced pet foods are actually less expensive than discount dog and cat foods. Higher quality of ingredients means the pet needs to consume less of the food to obtain necessary nutrition. Take a calculator to the pet store yourself. Definitely don't believe what Consumer Reports is trying to make you believe.

The Consumer Reports article *continues: "Most experts said individual ingredients are much less important than overall nutrient profile."* Nutrient profile? Since there is no "*nutrient profile*" category listed on any pet food label, we have to assume the Consumer Reports experts meant to say guaranteed analysis. Furthermore, no, neither the guaranteed analysis nor the nutrient profile are more important than ingredients.

Compliments of the FDA and AAFCO (American Association of Feed Control Officials), dog foods and cat foods must contain a minimum of various nutrients such as protein. However, regulations allow practically anything to be the source of these nutrients. As an example, let's look at pet food protein. An adult maintenance dog food must contain at least 18%

protein. An adult maintenance cat food must contain at least 26% protein. Thanks to misleading advertising and misinformed articles such as the Consumer Reports article, pet owners are led to believe protein means meat. However, pet food regulations state protein can be found in corn, chicken feet, and even in diseased or euthanized animals (and the lethal drug used to kill them). As long as an adult maintenance dog food analyzes as 18% protein and an adult maintenance cat food analyzes as 26% protein, very little attention is given to where that protein comes from. Whether high quality meat or diseased, decaying animals all analyze as protein. Nutrient profile or guaranteed analysis provides a petsumer with NO information as to the quality of the nutrition provided.

Opposed to what Consumer Reports tells pet owners, ingredients DO tell a great deal to petsumers. Common pet food ingredients "*animal fat*", "*meat and bone meal*", "*meat meal*", "*animal digest*", and "*by-product meal*" all provide protein to a dog food or cat food, yet they can contain rendered, (cooked) diseased, decaying, and drugged animals. Although pet food ingredients containing diseased, decaying, and drugged animals should be in violation of the Food, Drug, and Cosmetic Act laws, the FDA has ignored federal laws and allowed their use in pet food. Don't "*buy*" what Consumer Reports is selling you. Ingredients and quality of ingredients matter a great deal to your pet's overall health.

The next piece of misleading and incorrect information provided by Consumer Reports advises pet owners to look for labels stating that the food's nutritional adequacy was validated by animal-feeding tests based on protocols from the American Association of Feed Control Officials (AAFCO). The truth is that AAFCO's animal feeding trials could validate a highly inferior pet food quite easily. AAFCO regulations allow a dog food to be provided this certification (using the term certification lightly) after a 26 week test using 30 dogs. One fourth of the dogs can be removed from the final testing results if they don't meet the necessary good outcome. Along with some minimal blood testing, dogs cannot lose more than 15% of their initial body weight in order to provide the needed approval. Dogs are not required to be provided play and exercise as they would in a typical home. They can be crated with little to no activity in order to maintain body weight necessary for positive test results. Although some pet foods approved by feeding trials might be high quality, the regulations do NOT assure pet owners they are of any particular higher quality.

Another misleading point Consumer Reports is trying to sell pet owners regards health-promoting ingredients. *"There's some evidence that antioxidants — such as vitamin E — and some omega-3 fatty acids might enhance pets' immunity or help protect against certain diseases, but the experts interviewed by Consumer Reports were split on whether consumers need to look for them."* Some evidence? The truth is that there is a wealth of evidence that antioxidants and Omega 3 fatty acids benefit pets and help protect against disease. The Consumer Reports article seemed to be protecting the pet food manufacturers that choose profits over pet health, protecting pet foods that don't use health-promoting ingredients.

Although this could go on for days, there is one more point the Consumer Reports article used to mislead pet owners and seemed to protect some pet food manufacturing interests. They stated *"Most experts said they hadn't seen a pet get sick from inexpensive food; however, half said they had seen pets become ill from eating homemade pet food."*

If most "*experts*" have not seen a pet get sick from inexpensive food, perhaps these "experts" are blind to the skyrocketing increases in pet cancer, kidney disease, and liver disease. Inexpensive dog foods and cat foods come from inexpensive ingredient sources, risky chemicals and dyes. Science HAS linked the following inexpensive pet food ingredients to serious disease: ethoxyquin, BHA, BHT, menadione sodium bisulfate, BPA and many pet food dyes. Sadly, there is no scientific evidence that proves that foods containing diseased, decaying, and drugged animals cause disease or hinder optimal health. Such research is not necessary, however. There is no need to subject more pets to such hideous ingredients to conclude what any third grader could figure out given all the information. This is where the problem lies. Pet owners are NOT given all the information.

Articles such as this worthless piece from Consumer Reports and slick marketing tricks used by some pet food manufacturers continue to keep pet owners in the dark. Trusting pet owners see pictures of choice cuts of meat on a pet food label and assume steak or chicken breast is inside the bag or can. Many popular pet foods that provide pictures of steak or chicken breast on the label, actually contain the remains of diseased, decaying, and drugged animals, along with a mix of risky chemicals and dyes.

These so called experts quoted in the Consumer Reports article need to talk to pet owners, the real experts, who have changed their pet's diet to a high quality, meat-based pet food, naturally preserved, with a multitude of health promoting ingredients. These pet owners have seen the changes in their pets with their own eyes. Changes witnessed range from a shinier coat and increased activity to being able to stop hundreds of dollars of allergy treatments each month. Don't dare try to tell these experts that a high priced pet food that they bothered to learn contained high quality, health-promoting ingredients didn't make a difference in their pet. These pet food experts have living, healthy proof that high quality pet food makes a tremendous difference.

By the way, of the eight "experts" consulted by Consumer Reports, seven received funding from the pet food industry.

Pet Food Personal Experience - Misty, Holister & Frak

2006 was turning out to be a good year for my husband and me. We had a new home and a complete family, decent jobs, and we were happy, The family consisted of Misty, our 13 year old Lab/Collie mix that we had since she was six months old, our Holister, a 12 year old rescued Grey Hound that we had only had 2 years and loved intensely, two twin cat's Frik and Frak that we had for 16 years, and then the little one, Tex our youngest kitten at age 3.

In November Misty and Holister decided they didn't like their food any more. I had been feeding all our kid's Dry Nutro Max food for years. Starting in November I would open a new bag of food and they wouldn't touch it so I would "dress up" their food with gravies, people food, canned food, canned cat food, trying with anything in the world to get them to eat. Sometimes I would get a new bag of dry food and they would eat it, then they would decide they didn't like it again so out come's the canned food again. Misty, Holister and Frak all seemed to like the canned food selections and I could get them to eat so I thought it was okay because I was doing what was needed to take care of them.

The vet visits weren't real promising. Misty had been diagnosed with Congestive Heart Failure a couple of years earlier and was doing perfectly well on her med's. We had kept an eye on Holisters kidney values because Greyhounds are susceptible to kidney disease and he had not had any problems out of the norm. Frak had also been diagnosed with Heart disease a year before. These three kids are the one's that I fed canned food trying to get them to eat. The two kids we still have, Frik and Tex, didn't like the canned food so they ate dry Nutro cat food.

Then right at Christmas time Misty started getting sick. Trips to the vet got her fluids and blood work and changes of meds. We spent Christmas at home because we didn't want to leave Misty and Holister at a kennel since they weren't up to par. Little did we know it would be our last Christmas with Misty, Hollister and Frak. We all spent the day by the fire in the living room cuddled up in new blanket's Santa had left them for Christmas. Misty was a 90 pound dog in her day, but she was down to about 78 pounds at this time. On January 10th I called the Vet and he said to bring her in for fluid's to get her through the weekend. I, being a 110 pound weakling picked up my girl and put her in the car to get her down there because her dad was at work. She had one last weekend by the fire with us. On Monday she looked up at me and said Mom, it's time for me to go to heaven. So we let her go and our heart's broke, but we thought we understood.

Then Holister went downhill immediately. He wouldn't even get up out of bed for the next few days after Misty left. We knew he was grieving over the loss of his mate and didn't know what to do for him. We tried to get him out to walk and went to Pet Smart and tried to help him but he was totally depressed and totally wouldn't eat. I remember the last thing I succeeded in getting him to eat was a Junior Whataburger. The Vet couldn't figure out why he had cratered so fast. He was in kidney failure. Two weeks later Holister went to the Rainbow bridge with Misty.

My husband and I were totally devastated. Our kid's were gone and our sadness was deeper than the Grand Canyon. There was no barking, no running and playing and chasing the cats. No dog to let out in the yard to go pee. No dogs to feed. No reason to come home immediately after work to take care of the kids. We didn't do much but just exist in these first few months.

Then Frak started going down hill and losing weight. He refused to take med's the vet would give us. He wouldn't eat much and he would sit in the hall and meow a *really strange meow. Trying to tell us something was wrong. Fluids and steriod's helped some but only temporarily.*

Finally in March God put a new girl dog back into our lives. It was the only way for us to get out of the depression we were in. I left the house to go to the store on my normal Saturday errands and was going by the Denton Animal Shelter. The employee's had a little girl out in the yard and she caught my eye. I made a U-Turn in the street and went back and adopted her. I called my husband and told him I had found our new girl and both of us started crying all over again. She is a Golden Retriever Collie mix and God wanted her in our lives so we could love again. We named her Desire' (one long hoped for).

A week later God took Frak to the Rainbow Bridge. Frak got to where he couldn't breath. Desire' knew Frak was in trouble and sat with her nose on the bed watching him trying to let us know that she knew something was wrong. I think God knew we couldn't handle loosing another loved one so he made sure Desire' was here first.

Now Frik had to deal with the loss of his twin brother. They had been together all of their lives. It took him six month's to come around and finally adjust to the family changes and every day I hug this little guy, that just turned 17, and thank God for each and every day he gives to our family.

When we found out about the recall on the pet foods, it was too late. We had already lost two and the third was on his way down. Our vet would not say whether food was an issue for our kid's. But to loose all three of them in such a short period of time and they all had some of the recalled food has to have some connection. We've always taken better care of our kid's than ourselves. A year later we've finally paid off our vet bills. I still have some of the food in our home but our kiddos will never eat a Menu food product again. The devastation they have caused to so many pet families can never be rectified. I pray that Jay and his associates can change laws and make the big corporations realize that Pets ARE family members and ARE loved by their humans and no corporation should get away with Murder for the sake of their all mighty profits.

Curt and Danita C
Misty, Holister, Frik, Frak and Tex
Now
Frik, Tex and Desire'

Experts Speak Out

A panel meeting at the 2010 IFT (Institute of Food Technology) Annual Meeting & Food Expo "*encouraged pet food manufacturers to consider the health implications of their products in order to improve animals' health*" reports NaturalNews.com That's not likely, but…Wow!

Dr. Dressler, known as the "*dog cancer vet*" because of his work in unraveling the intricacies of canine cancer, said the key is severely limiting snack foods for humans and dogs that contain ingredients rich in Omega-6 fatty acids. Besides red meat common to some pet foods, other highly popular pet food ingredients such as soybean products, canola oil, and corn products produce Omega 6 fatty acids. "*Omega-6 fatty acids tend to increase inflammation, blood clotting and cell proliferation, while Omega-3 fatty acids decrease those functions of the immune system. The problem is that the typical American diet - for people as well as their pets - tends to be overloaded with Omega-6s and deficient in Omega-3s.*" (77)

From the IFT.org recap of the Healthier Pets Make for Healthier People presentation, "*Only 5–10% of cancers are attributable to genes. Consequently, the main factors affecting the rate of cancer in both humans and their pets are diet and lifestyle. Dressler says that three dietary factors leading to an increased risk of cancer are excessive consumption of Omega-6 polyunsaturated fatty acids (PUFAs), inefficient consumption of Omega-3 PUFAs, and excessive calories in food. Modern Western diets for humans have a 16 to 1 ratio of Omega-6 PUFAs to Omega-3 PUFAs. The same is true for pet food. This highly disproportionate ratio leads to inflammation, which provides an ideal environment for cancer. Tissue proliferation, blood supply, and cell movement also provide ideal conditions for cancer growth.*" (78)

The highest levels of Omega-3 fatty acid pet food ingredients are flaxseed or flaxseed oil, salmon, and fish oil.

Read your labels. Choose fewer soybean products, corn products, and canola oil and more flaxseed, salmon, and fish oil for a healthier you and a healthier pet!

A report from the Royal Veterinary College in London by Professor D.L. Chan points out that veterinarians should begin to look at nutrition to play a larger role in the health of pets. Similar to human doctors, most veterinarians don't write prescriptions of nutritional supplements for their pet patients. However, Professor Chan believes nutritional therapies need further veterinary exploration. The very first sentence of a recent paper published by Dr. Chan explains it all: "*Nutrition plays a critical role in the proper development and maintenance of optimal health in animals.*" Dr. Chan not only acknowledges the power of nutrition in maintaining optimal health in animals, but his paper also cites many clinical studies where nutrition actually improves and eliminates disease. (78)

One of the most promising nutritional supplements discussed by Dr. Chan is Omega-3 fatty acids. As we have seen, a source of Omega-3 is fish oil. Research has existed for years regarding maintaining good health by adding fish oil supplement to a human and animal diet. Dr. Chan quotes some very interesting research of Omega-3 actually treating and/or curing disease. He quotes a "*landmark study*" that demonstrated a diet enriched with Omega-3 greatly improved the health conditions of patients suffering from respiratory and lung disease.

Another amazing example of the power of fish oil is the brain recovery of Randal McCloy Jr., the only surviving coal miner in the 2006 Sage Mine disaster in West Virginia. After more than 40 hours of exposure to carbon monoxide, Randal McCloy "*had a massive heart attack from the carbon monoxide exposure, he was in kidney failure, liver failure, he was dehydrated, he was hypothermic, and he was in the deepest of coma.*" Neurosurgeon Dr. Julian Bailes and other doctors were "*uncertain if his brain would recover from its extensive injuries.*" Randal McCloy was given extremely high doses of fish oil and his brain functions started to improve. (79)

Dr. Barry Sears, a leading U.S. researcher of Omega-3 states fish oil is so remarkable because of its ability to reduce inflammation, especially "*silent inflammation*", which is "*below the perception of pain.*" Per Dr. Sears, silent inflammation is the first clinical sign that you are no longer well. Dr. Sears' website states that fish oil is the nutritional way to "*reduce silent inflammation. Then your state of wellness could be extended indefinitely.*" (80)

Unfortunately for pet owners and as stated in Dr. Chan's paper, very few studies are available for veterinarians researching diets enriched with fish oils treating critically ill pets. He states that human studies suggest "*a great potential to benefit such patients.*" However, research is readily available and vast on the health maintenance benefits of fish oil for humans and pets. Because of known contaminants, fish oil supplements for you or your pet should be of a pharmaceutical grade or very pure. Look for five-star-rated fish oils (five star being the purest) available at most health food stores. Be sure to ask the rating.

Antioxidants were the next topic. Dr. Chan's report suggested veterinarians incorporate antioxidants into animal health maintenance and treatments of disease. "*With the depletion of normal antioxidant defenses, the host is more vulnerable to free radical species and prone to cellular and sub-cellular damage (for example, DNA and mitochondrial damage). Replenishment of antioxidant defenses attempts to lessen the intensity of the signals that eventually leads to multiple organ dysfunction.*" Various studies of companion animals benefiting from antioxidants include improvement of congestive heart failure, pancreatitis, gastric and renal diseases.

The USDA's list of the top 20 food sources of antioxidants are small red beans, wild blueberries, red kidney beans, pinto beans, blueberries, cranberries, artichokes, blackberries, prunes, raspberries, strawberries, red delicious apples, Granny Smith apples, pecans, sweet cherries, black plums, russet potatoes, black beans, plums, and gala apples.

Lastly, the veterinarian-directed paper of Dr. Chan's reports on the importance of amino acids. "*Certain amino acids also serve as an energy source for certain cells; perhaps the most pertinent example being glutamine, which is the preferred fuel source for enterocytes and cells of the immune system.*" Studies have shown that in response to stress, "*there may be a dramatic increase in demand of particular amino acids and they must be obtained by the diet*". Recent studies have shown positive responses of the amino acid glutamine including cellular expression of "*heat shock proteins, which enable cells to withstand a great deal of injury and remain viable and functional.*" Dietary sources of L-glutamine include beef, chicken, fish, eggs, milk, dairy products, wheat, cabbage, beets, beans, spinach, and parsley.

Dr. Chan continues on the importance of glutamine, "*As the gastrointestinal tract is in fact the largest immune organ, dysregulation of the immune response further compromises the host and leads to multiple organ dysfunction. Given the relationship between critical illness and gut atrophy, supplementation with the gastrointestinal tract's preferred energy source, glutamine, is an attempt at restoring the integrity and function of this vital organ system.*"

While more than likely it will be years before veterinarians as a group begin utilizing nutritional therapies to treat disease and illness in our pets, the above research can be put to good use by pet owners to maintain the health of their pets. A health-promoting pet food provided to your dog or cat needs to provide quality meats, supplemented with Omega-3 and antioxidants. Call the pet food manufacturer and obtain their assurance that meats provided in the pet food are human grade/quality and look for several different quality meat proteins in the pet food. Also look for berries and other antioxidant-providing ingredients on the pet food label, and look for fish meal or fish oil ingredients. Avoid pet treats that don't provide the same health-promoting ingredients. An alternative would be to give your dog treats of apple slices and your cat canned pumpkin since both are natural sources of antioxidants. Add fish oil supplements to your pet's diet on a daily basis. Science has proven the tremendous benefits of these foods and food supplements so let your pet show you how well they work!

When the Unimaginable Happens - Tylenol

I'm guessing you've heard about the Tylenol recall, but you might not have read the fine print as to why some Tylenol products were recalled. This particular recall speaks volumes, should speak volumes to the FDA. Furthermore, the lesson provided by the Tylenol recall should send consumers screaming at the FDA to stop allowing adulterated pet foods to be sold right next to your food at your local grocery.

McNeil Consumer Healthcare voluntarily recalled certain lots of Tylenol on January 14, 2010. The company learned from consumer complaints of *"unusual moldy, musty, or mildew-like odor that, in a small number of cases, was associated with temporary and non-serious gastrointestinal events."* Upon investigation, McNeil Consumer Healthcare discovered *"that the reported uncharacteristic smell is caused by the presence of trace amounts of a chemical called 2,4,6-tribromoanisole (TBA). This can result from the breakdown of a chemical that is sometimes applied to wood that is used to build wood pallets that transport and store product packaging materials."* (81)

In other words, a chemical in the wood pallets that the Tylenol packaging was shipped on contaminated the product. The contamination was initially spread to product packaging long before any Tylenol was placed in each container and the container into the packaging) and, in turn, the contamination spread to the actual product. This one small chemical so far detached from Tylenol itself and which, prior to this valuable lesson was never even considered to be able to adulterate the final product, did exactly that!.

Understanding that one tiny chemical in the wood shipping pallets later contaminated the final product, we see that this actually CAN happen and, in fact, DID happen. Consider this:

Four D animals; Dead, Dying, Diseased, and Disabled animals. Cancer tumors, drug injection sites cut away from slaughtered meat-producing animals. Maggots, parasites, feces, rodents. Expired grocery store meat, used restaurant grease, road kill. Mix in euthanized dogs and cats from hundreds of thousands of animal shelters and veterinary hospitals and the lethal drug used to kill them. Rendered (cooked), then sold to pet food, cosmetics, and even crayon manufacturers.

Although the Federal Food, Drug, and Cosmetic Act clearly states that any food, human or animal, would be deemed adulterated and thus prohibited if it contains ANY part of a diseased animal or an animal that has died other than by slaughter, the FDA allows these horrendous ingredients to become pet food ingredients. *"Pet food consisting of material from diseased animals or animals which have died otherwise than by slaughter, which is in violation of 402(a)(5) will not ordinarily be actionable, if it is not otherwise in violation of the law. It will be considered fit for animal consumption."* (82)

So, again, understanding that the formerly believed-to-be-impossible scenario of one tiny chemical in the wood shipping pallets later contaminating the final product actually DID happen, how do you feel about your food sitting on a wood pallet next to pet foods that contain rendered, diseased animals, maggots, drugs, and cancerous tumors?

Right now, in hundreds of warehouses across the country, pet foods that contain rendered, diseased animals are sitting on wood pallets right next to your breakfast cereal and dried pasta, organic or not.

So how's that make ya feel? Furious? Me, too!

Is there a possibility that some contaminant from the rendered, diseased animals, maggots, drugs, and cancerous tumors could contaminate your food? Well, let's put it this way. Prior to the Tylenol recall, there could have been a good argument made against this ever happening, though I wouldn't have believed it! Now the FDA's argument has been greatly discounted. For the FDA to continue to state that its compliance policy which allows 4D animals to be processed into pet food is safe is simply ignorant. If a tiny chemical in wood pallets can leach into the packaging and then into the product (Tylenol), it is simply ignorant to continue to believe that diseased, rendered animals in pet foods eventually won't do the same; not even taking into consideration the quality of nutrition these ingredients provide to the pets that consume them, not even taking into consideration that these pet foods violate federal law each and every time they are sold to an unknowing consumer.

Will the FDA learn anything from the Tylenol recall? My fingers are crossed, but I'm not counting on it.

Salmonella

MSNBC.com told readers (8/25/10) "*The producers responsible for a recall of some 550 million potentially tainted eggs have found another outlet for the inventory that just keeps coming: They'll turn them into liquid eggs used in everything from cookies and cakes to egg substitutes and pet food.*" (83)

Yes, the millions of recalled eggs that should be destroyed will turn up in pet foods.

Feline Pride Salmonella Recall
Recently, a salmonella recall was announced by raw cat food producer Feline Pride. In numerous conversations with the president of the company, I learned that Feline Pride did exactly what the FDA instructed the pet food company to do. "*When producing a raw cat food, the only FDA requirement is to use USDA (United States Department of Agriculture) approved meat.*"

But, FDA tests found the raw cat food tested positive for salmonella. What happened? It seems the USDA happened!

In a phone conversation with the USDA, I was told "*USDA assumes all meat that leaves a USDA facility to be contaminated with salmonella*". The USDA informed me that their concern is not salmonella. Isn't that comforting? Isn't it comforting to think that every piece of meat in the grocery, your grocery, is assumed by the USDA to be contaminated with salmonella? No, it's not comforting!

What the American Veterinary Association Tells Pet Owners regarding Salmonella...

Dr. Ron DeHaven, Chief Executive Officer at the American Veterinary Medical Association, is the star of a recently produced video hosted on YouTube. The following are direct quotes from Dr. DeHaven:

"*Wash your hands after handling pet food and pet treats.*"
"*Don't allow immune-compromised young or old to handle pet food or treats.*"

"Keep your pets food and treats in a separate area from your food."

"Don't prepare your pet's food in the same area and certainly not with the same utensils (as your food)."

"Keep pets off countertops where your food is prepared."

"Feed your pet as far away from the human food preparation area as you can."

Ridiculous, isn't it?

How to avoid Salmonella contamination when feeding your pet

Good Morning America provided viewers with a story recently regarding three years of salmonella (strain Schwarzengrund) infecting consumers linked to dry pet food. The study quoted by GMA (and numerous other news outlets) was published by Pediatrics.org. The abstract of this salmonella investigation refers to *"manufacturer X dry dog food"*. The study does not state who *"manufacturer X"* is, but there are some clear hints.

"The outbreak strain was isolated from opened bags of dry dog food produced at plant X, fecal specimens from dogs that ate manufacturer X dry dog food, and an environmental sample and unopened bags of dog and cat foods from plant X. More than 23,000 tons of pet foods were recalled. After additional outbreak-linked illnesses were

identified during 2008, the company recalled 105 brands of dry pet food and permanently closed plant X." (84)

Mars Petcare recalled numerous brands of pet food during the time frame of the salmonella investigation. In November 2008, Mars Petcare announced that numerous brands of dog and cat foods produced at their Allentown, PA facility were being recalled. (85)

From the Center for Disease Control website: "*After additional outbreak-linked illnesses were identified in 2008, FDA conducted another investigation. In August 2008, FDA found the outbreak strain of S. Schwarzengrund in multiple brands of finished product at the plant, prompting another recall of products by Mars Petcare US. On September 12, the company announced a nationwide voluntary recall of all dry dog and cat food products produced at the Everson plant from February 18 to July 29, 2008, when production again was suspended at the plant. In addition, Mars Petcare US has taken steps to ensure that recalled products are no longer on store shelves. On October 1, the company announced that the Everson plant would be closed permanently. The FDA investigation is continuing.*" (86)

There was also a recall of Pedigree Dog Food due to this same strain of salmonella. (87) However, the FDA Pet Food recall page does not list Pedigree for any recalls. (88)

Ok, so we would have to assume that pet food 'manufacturer X' is Mars Petcare. Although the plant closed, the real reason for the salmonella contamination was never determined or at least was never announced to the public.

Spurred by an observant pet owner who contacted the blog EFoodAlert, food safety microbiologist Phyllis Entis did some investigative work into the latest batch of salmonella pet food recalls. Her investigation wondered if perhaps these various new recalls were linked to the hydrolyzed vegetable protein (HVP) recall that was initiated in early 2010 from Basic Food Flavors, Inc. (89)

The EFoodAlert blog states: "*Hydrolyzed vegetable protein (HVP) is used as a flavoring agent and likely would be sprayed over the kibble at the last stage of manufacture, after the cooking steps. Any salmonella that was present in the HVP would be transferred to the kibble.*"

But, Ms. Entis was unable to make the link of new pet food salmonella recalls to the recalled HVP. Why? Because no one would talk. She asked for answers to the possible HVP link and the recent salmonella pet food recalls but has received no answers from involved individuals. Ms. Entis requested information from Proctor & Gamble, Natural Balance, United Pet Group, and Merrick Pet Care. Below is what she was told:

1.   *Procter & Gamble: "In conjunction with the FDA, we are still investigating and therefore cannot provide further information at this time," replied Jason Taylor of P&G Pet Care External Relations.*

2.   *Natural Balance: "Please know that all information regarding the voluntary recall is available on our website," wrote Kristi Choy, Customer Service Manager, Animal Nutrition.*

3.   *United Pet Group: No reply.*

4.   *Merrick Pet Care: No reply.*

And the FDA isn't answering Ms. Entis's request for information either. She was told a Freedom of Information Act request would need to be filed for that information (the particular strain of salmonella in recent recalls). (90)

As of this writing, the FDA mentions no pet food recalls containing HVPs. (91)

But...many pet foods, treats, and bones DO contain flavor enhancers such as HVPs. The recalled pet food by Mars Petcare during 2008 and 2009 all contained 'Natural Flavors' (assumed to be some type of Hydrolyzed Vegetable Protein). The latest recall by Natural Balance, the pet food contains 'Natural Flavors'. The latest recall by Iams and Eukanuba, the pet foods involved all contain 'Natural Flavors'.

Is it possible that these latest Salmonella pet food recalls is due to FDA finally tracking down where Basic Food Flavors HVPs went? Is the FDA testing pet foods they know to contain the recalled HVP? The answer could lie in what type of Salmonella strain was found in these recent pet food/treat recalls. But remember, no one is talking about that.

I tried to discover the strain of Salmonella with no luck. A phone call to Iams/Eukanuba provided no answers. A P&G Customer Service Representative told me 'we are not releasing that information'. 'Bev

VanZant' with P&G Customer Service has emailed TruthaboutPet-Food.com of late the recent press releases, she emailed me "*We have requested the analysis from the FDA but have not received the data.*" A phone call to Merrick Pet Food Customer Service told me someone would return my call with that information. At the end of the day, about six hours later, no phone call. Natural Balance Pet Food told me "*It was an uncommon strain (of salmonella) not found in pet foods before*" but they would not provide me with the specific strain.

Flavoring remains the biggest connection with kibble pet food recalls due to salmonella. The recent story on Good Morning America implies flavoring was responsible for the salmonella-contaminated pet foods studied by Pediatrics Journal in what was assumed to be Mars Petcare products.

"*Salmonella contamination usually begins in the factory where pet food is made. According to ABC News senior health and medical editor Dr. Richard Besser, after the dog or cat food is processed, it is sent to a special room where the food pellets are coated with flavoring to make them taste good. Because this room is moist, it's a perfect environment for salmonella to grow,*" said Besser. "*And that salmonella can live on those food pellets for months.*" (92)

Flavoring. Now for the bad news. Almost every brand of kibble dog food and cat food contains "*flavoring*".

If there is no connection to the recent batch of salmonella pet food recalls and the Basic Food Flavors recalled HVP of early 2010, there remains the connection of pet food flavoring. Will we ever learn why/how these foods were contaminated with salmonella or how it can be prevented in these and other pet foods in the future? We should know these things, but...

Skeeter
March 16, 1994 - April 27, 2008

My 14-year old Chihuahua, Skeeter, was on Royal Canin Heart Disease food as prescribed by my vet when it was recalled because of contamination with melamine. Although her food was changed at that time, a few months later she passed from kidney failure. I have no doubt the melamine did not do her kidneys any good.

My experience with Skeeter has taught me to take actions in an attempt to prevent this same thing from happening again. I now buy 4 or 5 different brands of premium dog food with no grains, both canned and dry. I either mix or rotate them. If one has an ingredient that is going to harm the dogs, hopefully the other brands will dilute the harmful effects of it. And if one is lacking in a nutrient, the others may make up for it. With our dog food industry the way it is now, I think variety is the way to go. In addition to the various brands of commercial dog food I also supplement with home cooking and bites of "people food" as long as it's not junk food. I learned my lesson.

Christine, Lucy, Snoopy & Gizmo (fosters Maxine, Lilly, Chuy).

"Best By" Date

A pet owner's Yorkie became ill. After the dog spent a couple of days in the vet's office, the owner looked at her Eukanuba canned food and realized it had expired 3 years earlier. When she checked the cupboard, she discovered several other cans of dog food, all recently purchased at PetCo, that had expiration dates from 2004. (93)

What happened to this pet owner and pet can easily happen to anyone. How many times have you purchased something and never looked at the expiration date?

With pet food, somewhere on the can or bag (usually on the side or back of the bag) is the "*Best By*" date. Most of the manufacturers with whom I have spoken say that this date does NOT mean the food has officially expired. It just means that the food does not provide the optimal nutrition as stated in the guaranteed analysis. The "*best*" nutrition for your pet has expired but, in most cases, the food is still good, say the manufacturers.

Shelf life is one of the questions I ask manufacturers about and share that information in Petsumer Report. It varies greatly from manufacturer to manufacturer. The shelf life of dry pet foods can vary from 4 months to 3 years. Canned and/or pouched products vary from 1 year to 5 years. Treats usually have the same shelf life as the manufacturer's dry food but just to keep things confusing, that can vary too. The "*Best By*" date provided on the food does NOT tell you how old the product is. It does NOT tell you when the food was manufactured. It only tells you the date that this particular manufacturer has determined to be when the food no longer provides optimal and proper nutrition. While some ingredients in the food might still provide adequate nutrition, other ingredients may have faded over time.

All pet foods that are naturally preserved begin to lose their nutritional value almost immediately after they are made. This is the drawback to natural preservatives but it is the ONLY drawback. You ONLY want naturally preserved pet foods and treats for your pet. So the challenge is to find a pet food that is very fresh. Our friends at AAFCO (American

Association of Feed Control Officials), the "*rule makers*" of the pet food industry, have made that a little difficult for pet owners, adding to the challenge. Pet food manufacturers are not required to put the date the pet food was manufactured on the bag or can. They are required ONLY to put the date that that particular manufacturer has determined the food no longer is "*best*". As I stated above, this varies a great deal from product to product, manufacturer to manufacturer.

So here's what you can do to assure that your pet is eating ONLY fresh food, food that provides the best nutrition that product offers: Call the manufacturer and ask them what the shelf life is for their dry foods and/or canned foods. Let's say ABC Pet Food Company tells you that the shelf life of their Premium ABC dry foods is 18 months and their Premium ABC canned/pouched food is 2 years. With that information, you then look at the "*Best By*" date on the product. As an example, if the "*Best By*" date on the dry dog food you are considering says June 2011 and knowing that ABC told you that 18 months is the "*Best By*" date for their dry food, you would know that the food was made in December of 2009. Using today's date as January 26, 2011, would tell you that this particular bag of ABC dry dog food is 13 months old.

With a canned food, the ABC canned cat food "*Best By*" date is also June of 2011. This would tell you that this can was made in June of 2009 and thus it would be 19 months old in January of 2011. Most of the time, when pet owners look at the "*Best By*" date and they see June 2011, they think "*This is good. This food still has 8 months until it expires.*" I was guilty of this until I learned the differences too. But the bigger picture needs to be explained.

Using my above examples, I would NOT purchase a dry dog or cat food that was already 19 months old. Ideally, dry foods should be four months old or less and you should use them within a two month time frame. Again, with any naturally preserved dry product, the nutritional value starts to deteriorate almost immediately. Fresh is best. I recommend purchasing and using the food within six months of manufacturing. Storing the food in an airtight container will help keep the food fresher after opening the bag, providing your pet with more quality nutrition. With canned products, it's a different ballgame. You definitely want to purchase and use the food before the "*Best By*" date expires but the quality of the nutrition is protected by the canning process. Any unused, opened can must be covered and stored in the refrigerator and used within a couple of days.

Call your pet food's manufacturer and ask them the shelf life of their dry foods and canned foods. I know it's a chore, just one more thing you have to do and look out for, but it is very important. You want what you pay for – quality nutrition for your pet – and a fresh product will provide that. Of course you have to pay attention to ingredients too but that is a whole different subject!. Get yourself into the habit of looking at the "*Best By*" date BEFORE you purchase the pet food or treat. Your effort will not only provide your pet with better nutrition, it will also get you into the habit of looking at the expiration date. This could save you from an experience like the pet owner at the beginning of this section and a very sick pet!

Weight Loss Pet Food

The Journal of the American Veterinary Medical Association recently published the results of its diet/weight loss pet food study. Drs. Deborah Linder, DVM and Lisa Freeman, DVM took a close look at weight loss pet food. Their results shine a bright light on more misgivings about pet food.

Pet obesity is clearly a problem. It is reported that between 22% and 44% of dogs and cats in the U.S. are overweight or obese. Serious illness including pancreatitis, arthritis, diabetes and others are associated with overweight pets. Concerned pet owners turn to diet/weight loss pet food. However, Drs. Linder and Freeman's study shows that calorie intake, feeding instructions and the cost of diet pet foods is so conflicting and varied that weight loss pet foods could be adding to the pet obesity problem.

The study looked at two different categories of pet foods: (1) *"diets with weight management claims and feeding directions for weight loss"* and (2) *"diets with weight management claims on the label but no specific feeding directions for weight loss."*

In one category, 72 weight loss diets were examined that provided pet owners feeding directions to achieve weight loss, 40 dog diets (30 dry and 10 canned foods) and 32 cat diets (24 dry and 8 canned foods). Both over the counter weight loss foods and veterinarian prescribed pet foods were examined. The study found that 58% of this weight loss pet food group exceeded AAFCO calorie maximum allowances to make weight loss or lite (light) claims.

AAFCO calorie maximums for weight loss food:

Dry Dog Food	less than 3,100 kcal/kg
Can Dog Food	less than 900 kcal/kg
Dry Cat Food	less than 3,250 kcal/kg
Can Cat Food	less than 950 kcal/kg

Despite AAFCO regulations, the study found calorie counts in the following ranges for weight loss pet foods that provide feeding instructions specific to weight loss:

Dry Dog Foods	from 2,726 to 3,875 kcal/kg (almost 800 kcal over AAFCO allowances)
Can Dog Foods	from 553 to 1,002 kcal/kg (100 kcal over AAFCO allowances
Dry Cat Foods	from 3,018, 4,009 kcal/kg (750 kcal over AAFCO allowances)
Can Cat Foods	from 744 to 1,010 kcal/kg (60 kcal over AAFCO allowances)

The median (average) kcal/kg for this group of dry (kibble) weight loss pet foods were all above AAFCO allowances:

Dry Dog Food	3,295
Can Dog Food	857
Dry Cat Food	3,466
Can Cat Food	941

Cost of these pet foods varied greatly as well. Drs. Linder and Freeman found weight loss pet foods ranging from $0.53 to $4.66 per pound.

In the second category, 21 pet foods that stated weight loss claims that did not offer feeding instructions for weight loss provided similar results:

AAFCO calorie maximums for weight loss foods…

Dry Dog Food	less than 3,100 kcal/kg
Can Dog Food	less than 900 kcal/kg
Dry Cat Food	less than 3,250 kcal/kg

Can Cat Food	less than 950 kcal/kg
Dry Dog Food	from 3,065 to 3,615 kcal/kg Average 3,611 kcal/kg
Can Dog Food	(no range provided) Average 871 kcal/kg
Can Cat Food	from 916 to 1,096 kcal/kg Average 937 kcal/kg
Dry Cat Food	from 3,143 to 4,017 kcal/kg Average 3,473 kcal/kg

Pet food prices in this category ranged from $0.53 to $4.32 per pound.

So what are we left with from this study? Mass confusion if you happen to be a pet owner with an overweight pet! Drs. Linder and Freeman did a fantastic job pointing out the train wreck of weight loss options for pet owners. (My thanks to both of you for this study!).

The point is well taken that overweight pets are at risk for serious illness. However, with misleading pet food labels, no enforcement of pet food regulations regarding calorie allowances, and poor to no feeding instructions for weight loss, add to the dilemma veterinarians receiving the same mixed messages from pet food labels. How in the world can an overweight pet actually lose weight?

There is no Weight Watchers, Jenny Craig or NutriSystem for pets. Neither AAFCO nor the FDA is going to jump to the rescue of overweight pets. It's up to us. Pet owners of overweight pets MUST read the calorie (kcal) information on the pet food bag (or call the manufacturer and ask) and learn the kcal information for every treat we give our pets! Additionally, although we might find it challenging to add one more thing to our "*to do*" list, exercising our pets is an absolute MUST.

Treats

Don't give your pet treats. Give them a bonus!

We all do it. We give our pets treats as rewards or just because we love them. And many times pet owners don't think about the extra calories in treats or, worse yet, don't consider if the treat contains harmful ingredients. "*It's a treat. It won't hurt anything.*" Right? Well, it could! Dog and cat treats are NOT required to meet the nutritional standards of pet food and many, many are nothing more than junk food for pets. They add useless calories and potentially dangerous ingredients to their diet. So please don't give your pet a treat! Give them a bonus. A bonus contains added nutrients and health-promoting ingredients that even their pet food can't provide or provide enough of. A bonus can add these health-promoting benefits to your pet's diet and many of them do this in a low fat/low calorie fashion.

Poor quality treats contribute to the obesity problem in pets. I've talked to many pet owners who have been told by their veterinarian that their pet needs to lose a few pounds. Yet owners forget about the contribution that a handful of treats adds to the weight problem. Right along with weight issues is the fact that many treats are made using by-products and chemical preservatives and include ingredients that are difficult for the pet to digest. You might be feeding your dog or cat the right food but they still show signs of being overweight or have digestion and/or allergy issues. It could be that you have forgotten to look at the ingredients in treats. And good marketing helps to sway pet owners away from even thinking about looking at ingredients!

A few months ago, I went to one of the pet super stores to browse the dog and cat treats just to see what they offered. A mom and her two sons with dog in tow were searching for dog treats. The only ones that caught their attention were treats that had some type of human food connection like "*ribs*", "*bacon*", and so forth. Never once did they look at the ingredients on the "*ribs*" or "*bacon*" treat. I did... and every single variety they picked out contained by-products and BHA, BHT, or ethoxyquin. Pet treat marketing had lured them into a comfort zone of thinking that treats with names like "*ribs*" and "*bacon*" were as safe as human food. Again, every single treat this family picked out contained by-products and chemical preservatives linked to cancer. Pet owners must look at the ingredients of everything they feed their pets. Treat manufacturers are NOT going to alert you that they use risky ingredients. As you would guess, treats with names like "*Chicken Feet Dog Treats*", "*Cow Intestines Cat Treats*", or "*Cancer Causing Chemical Treats*" won't be top sellers! More treats than you realize contain all three of these undesirable ingredients.

Read those labels regardless of what the name of the dog treat or cat treat implies. Avoid treats that contain the ingredients "*by-product*", "*meat and bone meal*", "*animal digest*", "*BHA*", "*BHT*", and "*ethoxyquin*". (This is the short list.) Look for health-promoting ingredients like antioxidants and omegas from natural sources and as supplements. Don't forget about some "*people food*" bonuses. Carrots, green beans, and apple slices make great treats for dogs and even for some cats! Canned pumpkin makes a great, healthy treat for cats. Always consult your veterinarian if you have a pet health condition or you have any questions or concerns.

Stop feeding treats! Give your pet a bonus instead!

Do You Know What This Symbol Means?

Radura

     This symbol is called a RADURA logo. Although it looks like it implies "*green*" or environmentally friendly, the truth is that this symbol means the food was irradiated. SustainableTable.org states, "*During irradiation, food is exposed to high doses of radiation in the form of gamma rays, X-rays or electron beams. Irradiation can kill nearly all bacteria in food, both good and bad, but has no effect on the infectious agent that causes mad cow disease, or on viruses, such as those that cause hepatitis or foot and mouth disease.*"

     What can irradiation do to food? You might want to ask a pet owner from Australia that question. In 2008, the irradiated pet food imported into Australia ended up killing pets!

     While the FDA says irradiation is safe, SustainableTable.org states, "*The long-term health consequences of eating irradiated food are still unknown. Irradiation creates a complex series of reactions that alter the molecular structure of food and create known carcinogens, including benzene, and other toxic chemicals, including toluene. In addition, by-products of irradiation, called 2-ACBs, which do not occur naturally in any food, have been linked to cancer in rats and genetic damage in human cells. Animals fed irradiated foods have died prematurely and suffered mutations, stillbirths, organ damage and nutritional deficiencies.*" (94)

     Look for the radiation "*flower*" on the label. Avoid purchasing pet products that include the RADURA symbol. Also, the RADURA symbol

169

can be in a variety of colors. Many, many popular pet treats are treated with irradiation. The RADURA symbol will be somewhere on the packaging. Look for it! Tell a friend.

Pet Food Personal Experience - Dodger

Dodger snuck into my life unexpectedly. I went to a shelter which was full of sick cats, as I found out later, with the intent of adopting a cat after the purchase of my first home. My family always had cats around when I was growing up and I missed that feline presence.

I chose to adopt a shy but gentle cat that was trapped in a cage in the corner all by himself and named him Crusher. I took Crusher out of the cage, let him wander around and followed him. At some point I realized I myself was being followed. I turned around and there was a little gray tabby with a white chin and red nose looking up at me with the name "Dodger" written on his flea collar in magic marker. It was fate. I said to him, "all right, you too".

Dodger then continued to follow me everywhere. He followed me to the basement while I was lifting dumbbells and would make me nervous as he sat under the weights. He followed me to the sit up mat and followed my head as it went up and down. I would take him out to a field for a walk and he would just follow me around. He would be with me when I was working on a project around the house, but he would never get under my feet because he would always dodge out of the way, hence his name. Losing him was like losing my shadow.

Dodger was not quite six years old when he died. He always had a sneezing and respiratory problem when I adopted him as a kitten. I could always hear his breathing and he would periodically sneeze with such a powerful discharge that it could land five feet up on to the wall. The veterinarian believed it to be the symptom of an ear polyp and suggested removing it, but I didn't want the chance of losing him under anesthesia or causing permanent damage and decided instead to replace the carpet with laminate and periodically touch up the wall paint. He seemed comfortable as he was.

Five years later, the polyp suddenly grew and hit his middle ear, causing him to lose his balance. The polyp then needed to be removed. I was shaking at the prospect that I would never see him again after the surgery, but the polyp was removed and he recovered his balance but was left with a permanent head tilt. It was also discovered that he was infected with Bordatella Bronchyaseptica, otherwise known as Kennel Cough. This was found accidentally as Dodger suddenly sneezed a huge chunk of discharge on the veterinarian's stainless steel table, enough to take a culture. The veterinarian had me try six or seven antibiotics. They never worked. Something else was going on here.

A few months later, Dodger started vomiting bile, was lethargic, and seemed not to be eating and was losing weight. It took me a while to realize this because I would leave a big double bowl of kibble for both cats and fill it when it got low, and I never knew if he was eating or not. I may have grown up with cats, but I sure didn't know how to take care of them.

The veterinarian said he had pneumonia. After the standard administration of a cocktail of pharmaceuticals and supplying Dodger with a vaporizer for a couple of weeks, back to veterinarian he went because he was still vomiting and continued to lose weight. I wanted the vet to insert a feeding tube so I could feed him manually, and he said that Dodger didn't need a feeding tube. He needed a transfusion because he was severely anemic and he was dying.

Once realizing that my vet could not help him, I transported Dodger to a large animal hospital located over an hour's drive away. They diagnosed him with cancerous Mast cells in his spleen. They gave him a blood transfusion and splenectomy. A feeding tube was attached to his stomach so that I could feed him through the tube with a syringe full of "prescription" food. I would do this several times a day. He would usually vomit it up. I tried smaller amounts but more often. He continued to vomit. He went back to the hospital seven times in two months because he continued to come down with pneumonia and would not respond to the feeding method.

This story could never do justice to the minute by minute roller coaster ride of the ups and downs, the hopes and disappointments we both experienced through the ordeal. His condition would get better and then suddenly take a turn for the worse and this predicament cycled back and forth every few days until one morning I woke to find him cold and immobile in a pile a vomit on the bathroom floor. I put him in the car and raced him to the hospital only to hear his last breath ten minutes before we arrived. An eleven pound cat was five pounds at the moment of his death.

Over the next year, there were so many questions as to what actually caused him to get sick and die the way he did. The veterinarians could not answer my questions, or at least, they did not want to speculate. I believe it was hepatic lipidosis (fatty liver) that ultimately did him in. This is a condition cats fall prey to if they don't eat for long periods of time. I based this conclusion on hours of internet research. In idle conversation with my family, my sister-in-law made a comment about raw food for cats, which sparked me to do further research regarding the multiple feeding options for cats and the quality (or lack of) the various brands of cat food. After a year of reading on the subject, I was convinced that the "premium" brand that I was feeding Dodger largely contributed to his poor health and ultimately assisted in killing him. He was a sick cat to begin with, but a natural and healthy diet over the course of his lifetime may have been enough to save him.

Michael C.

Pet Owners Can Influence Change

In September of 2009, TruthaboutPetFood.com alerted pet owners to fish meal ingredients in some pet foods preserved with ethoxyquin, a chemical preservative linked to serious illness. Now it seems one manufacturer of numerous brands has changed to an ethoxyquin-free fish meal. Did pet owners influence this manufacturer to switch to a naturally preserved fish meal in its foods?

I firmly believe that pet owner complaints to these various pet food lines is what prompted this wonderful change in their fish meal. Kudos to all of you! Power to the Pet People! My thank you goes out to these pet food companies for listening to the desires of informed pet owners!

However, as with almost any good news with pet food, there is more to the story. This naturally preserved fish meal change should have been an easy question for these manufacturers to answer. The bad news is that it wasn't and some of the responses even had a nasty tone to them!

This was the correspondence with one manufacturer...

Secret Shopper: *"I heard that XXXXX has changed to an ethoxyquin-free fish meal. Is this correct? Does XXXXX guarantee that your fish meal ingredients are ethoxyquin-free? What is the new preservative used?"*

XXXXX Pet Food: *"Unfortunately in today's pet industry, there are so many myths and misconceptions related to pet nutrition, ingredients and manufacturing practices that we find it important to help you better understand the subject. At XXXXX we are always about transparency and openness, offering factual information about our products.*

There has long been speculation and often misinformation relative to preservatives in pet foods. Much of this comes from internet blogs and chat rooms. The information is generally opinion without factual support. At XXXXX we strive to procure only the highest quality ingredients that are 100% natural and free from chemical preservatives.

All XXXXX products when produced are always naturally preserved utilizing Naturox as an anti-oxidant. Naturox, a registered trademark, is an all-natural free flowing anti-oxidant for use in the preservation of oils, fats, fat-soluble vitamins, flavors, aromas, carotenoids and other oxygen-sensitive material. Ethoxyquin is never used as an anti-oxidant during our manufacturing process, and we continually test other brands of pet food to make sure we are below tested levels or within standards of our category."

Did you catch the trick answer? *"All XXXXX products when produced are always naturally preserved utilizing Naturox as an anti-oxidant."* Key words in this response are *"when produced"*. Of course when this pet food is *"produced"* they don't use ethoxyquin or it would be required to be listed on the label. The Secret Shopper question wasn't *"What preservative is used when you manufacture the food?"* The question was *"Have you changed to an ethoxyquin-free fish meal?"* This question was not answered directly, so...follow up email...

Secret Shopper: *"Thank you for such a prompt response! I guess the question I have is your statement..."All XXXX products when produced are always naturally preserved utilizing Naturox". I understand that some fish meal suppliers, prior to XXXXX receiving the fish meal, use ethoxquin. That is my question specifically: Does your fish meal supplier use Naturox or ethoxyquin? Not specifically you but your supplier."*

XXXXX

Pet Food: *"Your (sic) Welcome"*

What? Again, the question was not answered. Third time's a charm?

Secret Shopper: *"Thank you for such a prompt response but you didn't answer my follow up question. I guess the question I have is your statement..."All XXXX products when produced are always naturally preserved utilizing Naturox". I understand that some fish meal suppliers, prior to XXXXX receiving the fish meal, use ethoxquin. That is my question specifically: Does your fish meal supplier use Naturox or ethoxyquin? Not specifically you but your supplier."*

XXXXX

Pet Food: *"Oh, I'm sorry. Yes, Naturox is the preservative used."*

This pet food company never did directly answer the Secret Shopper question. We have to guess they did not because doing so would have been an admission that at one point they did use an ethoxyquin-preserved fish meal (which was already hesitantly confirmed by the manufacturer). Interesting that this pet food company did provide the unsolicited information that blogs and chat rooms are to blame for misinformation and XXXX Pet Food is all "about transparency and openness". Transparency and openness if you ask the same question three times!

Two pet food companies quickly and openly stated they were changing to a Naturox-preserved fish meal in their foods. One even stated in correspondence that, "*We are now ethoxyquin-free*". Thank you to both of these companies for being straightforward and honest (the first time!).

And then another pet food company responded to the Secret Shopper question by pounding on a pet food retailer:

Secret Shopper: "*I heard that XXXXX has changed to an ethoxyquin-free fish meal. Is this correct? Does XXXXX guarantee that your fish meal ingredients are ethoxyquin-free? What is the new preservative used?*"

Pet Food XXXXX: "*We have recently become aware that a pet food retailer, XXXXX, has drafted a letter which has been posted on many holistic websites notifying their customers that they have, "temporarily removed XXXXX from their store". According to them they have confirmed with the manufacturer that these brands contain ethoxyquin.*

1.   First and foremost, to our knowledge, no person or persons from "XXXXX" have ever contacted XXXXX regarding ethoxyquin.

2.   XXXX does not add ethoxyquin to our foods.

3.   Contrary to statements circulating around the internet, ethoxyquin is not the only approved preservative for imported fish meal products. Many years ago, the U.S. Coast Guard (now under The Department of Homeland Security) approved an all-natural preservative called NaturOx, which is made by Kemin. XXXXX has always mandated that its vendors not use ethoxyquin in the preservation process.

4.   In recent years, given the increasing worldwide demand for fish (primarily human side) and fishmeal, vendors have been reluctant and/or unable to make specification demands from fishmeal suppliers because of high market demand. Natural disasters commencing with Katrina, followed by tsunamis in Asia, earthquakes in Chile and now oil leaks in the gulf, all have and will further contribute to a reduction of the available fish to support the worldwide market. As a consequence, our fishmeal vendors have been increasingly reluctant to provide us with assurances of the methods of preservation. We were faced with a similar situation a couple of years ago concerning salmon meal. Then, as in now, our vendors reached a similar predicament in that they could no longer confirm that our salmon was ocean caught and not farmed. Fortunately, back then there was a healthy alternative, Menhaden herring, which was equally if not more nutritious and beneficial as salmon. Since there are no healthy alternatives to fishmeal, we have chosen instead to find a reliable vendor who uses an exclusive network of fishmeal suppliers that do not use ethoxyquin as a preservative. This lengthy process began early last year and after the successful conclusion of more than 6 months of shelf stability studies we will commence using our new source on June 1st."

Okay. Why in the world this pet food company went off on this pet food retailer is beyond me. Perhaps they were thinking that if they make this retailer look bad in the eyes of the Secret Shopper, the Secret Shopper won't catch on to the rest of the garbage they were spouting!

The Secret Shopper question didn't ask this pet food if "*it*" added ethoxyquin, yet answer number two above provides that unsolicited information.

Answer number three? Nope, don't buy it. The truth is, when the first article about ethoxyquin in fish meal was published on Truthabout-PetFood.com, numerous pet owners forwarded me the response from this pet food manufacturer and others. These pet food companies were telling pet owners that ethoxyquin was the ONLY preservative allowed by federal law, not the other way around. (I've still got the emails should these pet food manufacturers wish to dispute this.) When unknowing pet owners wrote TruthaboutPetFood.com with these ridiculous lies from pet food companies, I provided the pet owner with the rest of the story about Naturox and federal regulations. Then we saw their response to pet owners change to "*there is not enough naturally preserved fish meal available*," another lie. (98)

The last sentence of answer number three, "*that XXXXX has always mandated that its vendors not use ethoxyquin in the preservation process*," is simply not correct. Their lie in number three is proven by their answer in number four.

After the blah, blah, blah list of distractions, this pet food almost openly admits to having once used an ethoxyquin-preserved fish meal in complete contradiction to their statement in number three. "*Since there are no healthy alternatives to fishmeal, we have chosen instead to find a reliable vendor who uses an exclusive network of fishmeal suppliers that do not use ethoxyquin as a preservative. This lengthy process began early last year and after the successful conclusion of more than 6 months of shelf stability studies we will commence using our new source on June 1st.*" This lengthy process began early last year? New source on June 1st? Wow, did you just point out that you lied in your previous statement?

While pet owners did a great thing by motivating these pet food companies to switch to a naturally preserved fish meal, we have a really long way to go as you can tell by some of their answers. If they would spend as much time searching for quality suppliers as they do searching for clever ways to avoid telling the truth to pet owners, we'd be so much better off!

In 2008, Pet Owners nationwide sent their Representatives in Congress the following letter. Only one (over 50 Representatives were contacted) bothered to even read the letter and request follow up information from FDA; the late Senator Robert Byrd. Every other elected Representative in Congress ignored these Pet Owners request for action.

"*Dear ,*

As a tax payer and a voting citizen, I am writing to inform you that the FDA is ignoring federal law. The FDA is blatantly allowing pet food manufacturers to ignore the U.S. Federal Food, Drug, and Cosmetic Act (FFDCA) and, in turn, many brands and varieties of pet foods are being shipped and sold all across the U.S. with misleading labels and adulterated ingredients. This deliberate law bending must stop.

To provide you with an understanding, the following are excerpts from the Federal Food, Drug, and Cosmetic Act. Section 201 (f) of the FFDCA plainly states the definition of food: "The term 'food' means (1) articles used for food or drink for man or other animals, (2) chewing gum, and (3) articles used for components of any such article." Section 301 plainly states prohibited acts: "The introduction or delivery for introduction into interstate commerce of any food, drug, device, or cosmetic that is adulterated or misbranded." (c) "The receipt in interstate commerce of any food, drug, device, or cosmetic that is adulterated or misbranded, and the delivery or proffered delivery thereof for pay or otherwise." And Section 402 defines adulterated food: "A food shall be

179

deemed to be adulterated (if it contains) (a) poisonous, unsanitary, or deleterious ingredients." (a)(5) "if it is, in whole or in part, the product of a diseased animal or of an animal which has died otherwise than by slaughter;"

The FDA has taken it upon itself to provide pet food manufacturers the ability to ignore Section 402 of the FFDCA. Below are direct quotes from the FDA website to prove this, along with the page locations.

"Pet food consisting of material from diseased animals or animals which have died otherwise than by slaughter, which is in violation of 402(a)(5) will not ordinarily be actionable, if it is not otherwise in violation of the law. It will be considered fit for animal consumption."

"The pet food canning industry utilizes undecomposed animal and marine tissues from various sources. These include products of the rendering industry such as various meat, poultry, and bone meals; meat scraps and offal from packing house waste; freshly boned-out animals; and occasionally meat from animals that may have died otherwise than by slaughter. Before processing, many of these commodities may be considered in violation of *402(a)(5)*; however, the Center for Veterinary Medicine (CVM) is aware of no instances of disease or other hazard occurring from canned packing house offal or the tissues of animals that may have died otherwise than by slaughter." http://www.fda.gov/ora/compliance_ref/cpg/cpgvet/cpg690-300.html

The Federal Food, Drug, and Cosmetic Act does NOT allow for diseased animals or animals which have died other than by slaughter into any food regardless of whether or not the "commodities" are processed. The FDA has, in essence, rewritten the laws that Congress developed to protect U.S. citizens and their pets. Does Congress approve of the FDA writing its own version of the law?

Whether the CVM is "aware of no instances of disease or other hazard" occurring from pets consuming foods which contain what is referred to as 4-D animals — dead, dying, diseased and disabled animals, the use of these 4-D animals is in direct violation of federal law. The very reason 4-D animals are not used in human food, the risk of disease, should be the very same reason they are not used in animal foods. The law provides this for U.S. consumers AND their pets.

Another page on the FDA website is in contradiction to their statements above. http://www.fda.gov/ora/compliance_ref/cpg/cpgvet/cpg690-500.html

"CVM is aware of the sale of dead, dying, disabled, or diseased (4-D) animals to salvagers for use as animal food. Meat from these carcasses is boned and the meat is packaged or frozen without heat processing. The raw, frozen meat is shipped for use by several industries, including pet food manufacturers, zoos, greyhound kennels, and mink ranches. This meat may present a potential health hazard to the animals that consume it and to the people who handle it."

The Center for Veterinary Management, instead of simply being "aware of the sale of 4-D animals for use as animal food," should be actively prosecuting each and every company that utilized animal food ingredients from dead, dying, disabled or diseased animals. Pet food ingredients that could contain a 4-D animal are some of the most popular pet food ingredients including "by-product meal" and "animal fat."

There have been rumors for many years that euthanized pets removed from countless animal shelters across the country have become rendered ingredients in pet food. In 2002, the FDA provided a report on its testing of dog food purchased directly from store shelves and found many of the foods contained pentobarbital, the drug used to euthanize animals, including pets and shelter animals. http://www.fda.gov/cvm/FOI/DFreport.htm

This report again proves the FDA allows euthanized animals, and the drug used to end their lives, to become pet food in direct violation of the FFDCA. The FDA has also determined the pet food ingredient "animal fat" to be the most likely ingredient to contain a euthanized animal and pentobarbital. "Animal fat" is commonly used by many of the top brands of pet foods today. The sale of, and the transport of, these pet foods is in violation of federal law.

Lastly, the FDA endorses mislabeling of pet foods by flatly accepting the pet food regulations developed by AAFCO, the American Association of Feed Control Officials. AAFCO regulations state: "Regulation PF7 of the AAFCO manual, category Nutritional Adequacy: (a) "The label of a pet food or specialty pet food which is intended for all life stages of the pet or specialty pet may include an unqualified claim, directly or indirectly, such as "complete and balanced," "perfect," "scientific" or "100% nutritious..." Yet the FFDCA states (Section 403): "A food shall be deemed to be misbranded, a 'false or misleading label' if (1) its labeling is false or misleading in any particular, or (2) in the case of a food to which section 411 applies, its advertising is false or misleading in a material respect or its labeling is in violation of section 411(b)(2). An 'unqualified claim, directly or indirectly' is false and misleading which is in direct violation of federal law.

I urge you to take an investigative trip to the pet food aisle at your local grocery store or pet store. There you will find a huge array of pet foods that the FDA allows to violate federal law. It is your job as a representative of both the United States of America and your state to stop this from happening. Please do not allow this to continue. Do not allow the FDA to shift the blame towards AAFCO or any other organization. The sole responsibility lies within the FDA to enforce federal law.

The FDA is ignoring federal law and it must stop immediately. No government agency should be allowed to ignore federal law. I am waiting for your response and 74 million U.S. pet owners are waiting for changes. We hope you make the right choice.

Sincerely,

_____ "

The next step pet owners took was to file a citizen petition with the FDA. A citizen petition is the FDA's official method to request that it alter existing regulation(s), in this case, a request to enforce federal law). Below is the citizen petition sent to the FDA with over 500 pet owner signatures attached.

Citizen Petition Received 8/5/10, docket number FDA-2010-P-0416-0001/CP

Division of Dockets Management
Food and Drug Administration
Department of Health and Human Services
5630 Fishers Lane, rm. 1061
Rockville, MD 20852

Citizen Petition

The undersigned submits this petition under Section 402 (a)(5) of the Federal Food, Drug, and Cosmetic Act to request the Commissioner of Food and Drugs to enforce existing law with pet foods and treats.

A. Action requested
Per Section 201 (f) of the Federal Food, Drug, and Cosmetic Act, "The term 'food' means (1) articles used for food or drink for man or other animals, (2) chewing

gum, and (3) articles used for components of any such article." Thus, pet food and treats are included in the definition of food within the act.

Section 402, Adulterated food, states "A food shall be deemed to be adulterated - (a) Poisonous, unsanitary, or deleterious ingredients." "(a)(5) if it is, in whole or in part, the product of a diseased animal or of an animal which has died otherwise than by slaughter;"

Section 301 of the act states Prohibited Acts and Penalties: (a)"The introduction or delivery for introduction into interstate commerce of any food, drug, device, or cosmetic that is adulterated or misbranded." "The receipt in interstate commerce of any food, drug, device, or cosmetic that is adulterated or misbranded, and the delivery or proffered delivery thereof for pay or otherwise."

Presently, FDA compliance policy states "POLICY: Pet food consisting of material from diseased animals or animals which have died otherwise than by slaughter, which is in violation of 402(a)(5) will not ordinarily be actionable, if it is not otherwise in violation of the law. It will be considered fit for animal consumption."

FDA compliance policy acknowledges violations of the Act in pet food. This Citizen Petition requests the Commissioner to enforce the Federal Food, Drug, and Cosmetic Act as it is written with respect to pet foods and treats.

Further, FDA allows pet foods that contain illegal ingredients sourced from diseased animals or animals that have died otherwise than by slaughter (labeled by FDA as "suitable for use in animal feed") to be marketed/sold to unknowing pet owning consumers as 'premium', 'choice', and a long list of pleasing terms. Section 403 of the Act states "A food shall be deemed to be misbranded- (a) False or misleading label. If (1) its labeling is false or misleading in any particular, or (2) in the case of a food to which section 411 applies, its advertising is false or misleading in a material respect or its labeling is in violation of section 411(b)(2)." Pet foods and treats that include ingredients sourced from diseased animals or animals that have died other than by slaughter, unless labeled as such (which of course there is none) would be a violation of labeling laws.

Petitioner(s) as well requests Commissioner to enforce all Food, Drug, and Cosmetic Act labeling laws for the safety and health of all pets.

B. Statement of grounds

183

The grounds of this request are Federal law; the Food, Drug, and Cosmetic Act. The Act clearly includes pet food/treats within the definition of food. The Act clearly deems a food to be adulterated and thus prohibited if it contains in whole or in part a diseased animal or an animal which has died other than by slaughter. FDA Compliance Policy states pet foods consisting of diseased animals or animals which have died other than by slaughter will not be actionable. This in itself is sufficient grounds to prove Federal laws are violated with some pet foods and treats.

Further, FDA report 'Risk of Pentobarbital in Dog Food' confirms some pet foods violate Federal Food, Drug, and Cosmetic Act. FDA testing found pentobarbital in dog food purchased off store shelves. Pentobarbital is used to euthanize dogs, cats, horses, and rarely cows. FDA testing confirming a euthanizing drug in dog food would/should deem those products adulterated; a violation of the Food, Drug, and Cosmetic Act.

Further, follow up FDA investigation determined that the common pet food ingredients "Meat and Bone Meal (MBM), Beef and Bone Meal (BBM), Animal Fat (AF), and Animal Digest (AD) are rendered or hydrolyzed from animal sources that could include euthanized animals." Based on this FDA research, any pet food or treat that contains meat and bone meal, beef and bone meal, animal fat, and/or animal digest could be adulterated according to the Act.

FDA commonly uses the term "suitable for use in Animal Feed".

Until the recent ban on BSE Specified Risk Material (SRM) in animal feed, even these risk and illegal materials were deemed 'suitable for use in animal feed' by FDA. Federal Food, Drug, and Cosmetic Act does not separate definition and regulation of suitable for use of human food and suitable for use in animal food. Definitions of food, adulterated food, and prohibited food within the Act covers all food, human and animal.

Petitioner(s) believes FDA does not have authority to override Federal law.

Various FDA/CVM documents make statement to CVM being unaware of any adverse health effects due to animals consuming pet foods/treats containing disease animals or animals that have died other than by slaughter. Regardless of such statements by CVM, Federal law states these types of pet food ingredients are illegal.

Petitioner(s) requests FDA to enforce all Federal Food, Drug, and Cosmetic Act laws with respect to pet foods and treats. Petitioner requests that all pet foods and treats containing FDA's determined pentobarbital risk ingredients (meat and bone meal, beef and bone meal, animal fat, and animal digest) to be removed from store shelves until manufacturer can provide complete and concise evidence ingredients are within the guidelines of the Food, Drug, and Cosmetic Act.

Petitioner requests that any pet food/treat manufacturer sourcing ingredients from 'dead stock' renderers and/or USDA rejected meat or meat products or 4D animals (rendered or otherwise) be considered adulteration high risk; requiring frequent FDA inspection and burden of evidence of compliance from the manufacturer.

C. Environmental impact

Petitioner(s) has no knowledge of environmental impact by FDA enforcing Federal Food, Drug, and Cosmetic Act. It is assumed however, that detailed environmental impact studies have previously shown no dramatic environmental impact when FDA enforces the Act. It is assumed that Congress would not have written and passed the Food, Drug, and Cosmetic Act - including the protection of pet food and treats - should a dangerous environmental impact be the outcome.

D. Economic impact

Petitioner(s) acknowledges the possibility of economic impact of industry. Petitioner(s) acknowledges the possibility of economic impact of pet owners.

The pet food ingredients meat and bone meal, beef and bone meal, animal fat, and/or animal digest (deemed by FDA testing to be most likely pet food ingredients to contain a euthanized animal) are used in many pet foods and treats in a variety of price categories. Various documents from related pet food industry businesses found on the FDA website discuss the economic impact to their industry when BSE Specified Risk Materials were banned from animal feed. Petitioner(s) would suspect that Rendering Industry, without the pet food/treat market as a sales outlet for ingredients sourced from diseased animals and animals that have died other than by slaughter, would suffer the greatest economic impact.

However, the economic impact to pet owners that unknowingly feed their dog or cat a food with ingredients sourced from diseased animals or animals that have died other than by slaughter must be considered as well. If meat or meat ingredients sourced from diseased animals or animals that have died other than by slaughter were considered nutritious and/or beneficial to the health of those that consume them, they would not be considered an adulterant by Federal Food, Drug, and Cosmetic Act. While there is no scientific evidence to prove pet foods/treats that contain an ingredient sourced from diseased animals or animals that have died other than by slaughter would have an adverse effect on the health of the pets that consume them, the Petitioner(s) takes a common sense approach. Common sense tells us because this type of meat ingredient is illegal according to Federal Food, Drug, and Cosmetic Act, Petitioner(s) believes these ingredients to be a risk to the health and longevity of pets. The long term health effects of a pet consuming such inferior and illegal ingredients could be quite costly in veterinarian care.

E. Certification
The undersigned list of concerned pet owners certifies, that, to the best knowledge and belief of the undersigned, this petition includes all information and views on which the petition relies, and that it includes representative data and information known to the petitioner which are unfavorable to the petition.

(Signature)
(Name of petitioner)
(Mailing address)
(Telephone number)

The petition was received by the FDA on August 5, 2010 and was assigned docket number FDA-2010-P-0416-001/CP.

The following is the response we've received from FDA...

January 28, 2011

Re: Docket No. FDA-2010-P-0416

Dear Ms. Thixton:

This is a tentative response to the Citizen Petition (FDA-2010-P-0416) filed with the Food and Drug Administration (FDA) on August 5, 2010. This petition requests the FDA to: enforce all Federal Food, Drug, and Cosmetic Act (FD&C Act) laws with respect to pet foods and pet treats; require the removal from store shelves of pet foods and treats containing certain ingredients until such time that the manufacturer provides evidence that those ingredients are within the guidelines of the FD&C Act; and consider certain pet food and pet treat manufacturers sourcing ingredients from specified sources adulteration to be high risk, thereby requiring frequent FDA inspection and burden of evidence of compliance from the manufacturer.

Pursuant to the administrative regulations at 21 CFR 10.30, FDA is required to respond to your petition within 180 days. FDA currently is considering the issues raised by your citizen petition. However, the agency will require additional time to issue a final response due to the existence of other agency priorities at this time. FDA will issue a final response to your citizen petition after completing the analyses of all the issues raised in the petition.

Sincerely yours,

Bernadette M. Dunham, D.V.M., Ph.D.
Director, Center for Veterinary Medicine

It could take years for the FDA to issue their final response.

Pet Food Recall First Alert

In 2007 melamine was the killer of countless dogs and cats across the U.S. and Canada. Today there is a new killer of pets; silence.

The 2007 pet food recall taught Pet Food and the FDA something BIG. The 2007 pet food recall taught Pet Food and the FDA that Pet Parents go a little ballistic over news of a pet food recall. It's been referred to as 'pet food hysteria'. Instead of just going on as usual, panicked 'hysterical' Pet Parents turned to blogging and Tweeting about a tainted pet food. We (pet parents) want to learn everything we can and want to share every bit of pet food news the best way we can hoping to save the life of our or someone else's pet. This blogging and Tweeting told Pet Food and the FDA pet parents have lost trust in pet foods and have serious doubts of the effectiveness of the FDA. The apparent new method of handling pet food recalls, is not handling them at all. The new recalls are silent.

Here are examples of 'silences' that have happened in pet food...

Premium Edge Pet Food learned of cats getting sick (one died) in the Rochester, NY area. The pet food manufacturer (Diamond Pet Foods) tracked down the food the sick cats had consumed; the company discovered all suspect foods were manufactured within a twelve minute time frame. It is believed that some type of manufacturing error occurred during those twelve minutes. Premium Edge contacted distributors and retailers in the Rochester area to pull suspect product from store shelves. No official recall was initiated with the FDA nor did Premium Edge add a press release to their website until after news broke publicly. The FDA recall came 18 days after the Premium Edge recall was published on TruthaboutPetFood.com. What happened to the pets that was already eating that cat food unknowingly?

Another recent pet food product pull was from Wysong. After a reported death of a dog, Wysong discovered mold in several lots of dog foods believed to be caused from a *"malfunctioning moisture checking device"* during manufacturing. The second Wysong statement told petsumers that incoming ingredients and finished products are tested for moisture and mycotoxins (mold). Despite stated testing, dog foods still managed to contain mold and still managed to be shipped to distributors and retail outlets. Wysong placed a press release on their website; however it was not easily found. No official recall press release was initiated by the FDA. In fact, Wysong stated the FDA told them a press release was not necessary. *"The matter was of small enough consequence that we have even been told by the FDA that a news release is not necessary."* (95)

Again, what happened to the pets that were eating the moldy foods sold previous to the dog food withdrawal? (Latest statement from Wysong (96))

Why was there not a prompt FDA recall press release of these pet foods? Why were these products (and others) 'withdrawn' from store shelves instead of publicly and promptly recalled? What is the difference between a pet food withdrawal and a pet food recall?

The FDA provided me the following explanation to the difference between a pet food withdrawal and a pet food recall..."*FDA does not have statutory authority to require manufacturers to initiate pet food recalls. Therefore, the initiation of such recalls on the part of manufacturers or importers is voluntary.*

Please see the following for additional information on recalls:
http://www.fda.gov/ForConsumers/ConsumerUpdates/ucm049070.htm

Recalls classified as Class I require a press release which is typically issued by the firm. FDA posts those releases at http://www.fda.gov/Safety/Recalls/default.htm.

Companies have conducted recalls that were not classified as Class I and issued press releases which is their prerogative but only Class I classified recalls require a press release."

The FDA website defines a Class I, Class II, and Class III recall as:
Class I: Dangerous or defective products that predictably could cause serious health problems or death. Examples include: food found to contain botulinum toxin, food with undeclared allergens, a label mix-up on a lifesaving drug, or a defective artificial heart valve.

Class II: Products that might cause a temporary health problem, or pose only a slight threat of a serious nature. Example: a drug that is under-strength but that is not used to treat life-threatening situations.

Class III: Products that are unlikely to cause any adverse health reaction, but that violate FDA labeling or manufacturing laws. Examples include: a minor container defect and lack of English labeling in a retail food. (97)

Now…the FDA states a Class I recall requires a press release. Class I is defined as a dangerous or defective product that predictably could cause serious health problems or death. Both of these recent pet food withdrawals are believed to have caused numerous serious illnesses and death, thus classifying them into a Class I recall. Yet neither of this pet food withdrawals were promptly released on the FDA website as is standard for Class I recalls. Why not?

The same FDA webpage states the following about recalls…
"*FDA seeks publicity about a recall only when it believes the public needs to be alerted to a serious hazard. When a recalled product has been widely distributed, the news media is a very effective way to reach large numbers of people. FDA can hold press*

conferences, issue press releases, and post updates to its Web site regularly, to alert people."

"It's about being as transparent as possible," says Catherine McDermott, public affairs manager in the Division of Federal-State Relations in FDA's Office of Regulatory Affairs. *"If we feel there is that much of a health risk, we will offer media updates every day to give new information, and all that we know gets posted to FDA's Web site."*

'Transparent'? Are you kidding me?

As if the above wasn't enough of a concern, there is one more pet food issue that must be addressed. When a pet food is withdrawn from store shelves, what about the customers that have already purchased that suspect food? Don't these pet owners deserve to be warned?

It's quite a problem. Pet Food doesn't like to admit an error has occurred with their pet foods. Who would? An official pet food recall becomes a permanent scar on the company image; furthermore it could become a haunting financial disaster.

However, on the other side of the coin, are pet owners... scared out of their wits. There is probably not a pet owner in the U.S. or Canada that doesn't have a first hand experience with a sick pet due to a pet food or know someone that does. Over the past several years, thousands of dogs and cats have died directly because of a pet food. Thousands of pet deaths, YET nothing has changed in pet food regulations to prevent future deaths. Pet owners are frightened; worried sick if their pet's food will recalled or silently pulled from store shelves...AFTER their dog or cat has been eating it. Will they learn the food is bad too late? Will their beloved dog or cat get sick or die?

There is a GAPING HOLE in the pet food withdrawal and recall system that everyone of authority seems to be ignoring; Notification to pet owners. Ya know...the people that purchased the pet food...they're called CUSTOMERS! Customers and their pets are falling into this GAPING HOLE and no one seems to care.

Thanks to the Internet and a world of concerned pet parents, news of pet food withdrawals does get out sooner or later…but I have to wonder how many times has the news of a suspect pet food arrived too late? How many pets have fallen into the GAPING HOLE? One sick pet due to NOT INFORMING A PET OWNER is too many.

Furthermore, with every new story of a pulled pet food, without first learning it from the pet food company itself…the suspicion meter rises. What else are they (pet food) hiding? What else are they not telling us? More and more pet owners become even more untrusting of ALL pet food.

Trying to keep the lid on a pet food withdrawal isn't working. The current recall system isn't working either.

So Pet Owners took matters into their own hands. We wrote our pet food manufacturers and asked them to join our consumer initiated Pet Food Recall First Alert program. Here's how the program works…

* Each participating Pet Food Company will agree to initiate an email alert system to promptly notify customers when/if a problem is discovered with a pet food; for customers that wish to be notified via voice mail, the Pet Food Company agrees to initiate a voice mail system as well.

× Once your Pet Food Company's notification system is up and running, Pet Parents can register at their Pet Food Company's website to be notified of a pet food recall or pet food product withdrawal.

× Each participating Pet Food Company will be listed on TruthaboutPetFood.com as a member of Pet Food Recall First Alert Program.

× Millions of Pet Food customers will be promptly notified of a recalled pet food; Millions of Pet Parents will see the final list; which Pet Food Companies have chosen integrity over secrecy.

Pet Owners sent the following letter/email to their pet food manufacturer…

Over the past several months, consumers have learned of numerous pet food withdrawals across the U.S. Pet foods were quietly pulled from store shelves due to sick and/or dying pets. The FDA didn't provide this information about potential bad pet food; consumers were forced to learn this information on their own.

We (pet owners) understand that human error happens; no company can guarantee their foods will be completely safe, every single batch, month after month and year after year. While no one wants to learn there is a problem with their pet food, what we REALLY don't like is learning of a silent pet food recall from Internet forums or blogs. On this note, we ask you to consider the following...

Should the worst happen and you need to recall or pull a pet food or treat from store shelves, we ask that you inform your customers directly. With the assistance of an email auto-responder program (such as Get-Response or Constant Contact) your customers can register for your alerts. A brief email can be sent to all of your registered customers with a click of a mouse, alerting them to stop feeding a recalled food. We ask that you alert all registered customers within 24 hours of your company's product pull or within 24 hours of your company's knowledge of a pet food problem. This small effort on your part can save the life of countless pets.

We also ask that you post a "warning" on the main page of your website to alert consumers of the lot numbers being recalled.

We are not asking for your Pet Food Company to ignore reporting a problem to regulatory authorities. We are simply asking that you promptly inform your customers directly should a problem with a pet food or pet treat occur. We are very aware that although the FDA initiates recall press releases, we know that many times pet owners do not learn of the recall until it is too late. This simple program can work together with the FDA to inform more pet owners when a problem occurs.

We (Pet Owners) call this program Pet Food Recall First Alert and we hope you consider participating. Again, all we are asking is that you inform your customers directly in a timely manner should a pet food recall or withdrawal occur via an email auto-responder system. We really do want to keep our pets safe and we want to learn of a problem from you — not from Internet blogs or forums.

Please respond to this email so that I (your customer) know my Pet Food Company is choosing integrity over secrecy. Also, please respond to Susan@TruthaboutPetFood.com. With your word that you will email customers directly, TruthaboutPetFood.com will add your name to the growing list of Pet Food Companies. Also, you will be provided the Member of Pet Food Recall First Alert logo to add to your website to show your customers and potential customers you are participating in this worthwhile program. We hope to see your name added to the list soon.

Thanking you in advance for your prompt cooperation.

Sincerely,

A devoted Pet Owner & your Customer

As of the printing of this book, here are the companies that have willingly joined us...

Nature's Logic Pet Food
Mulligan Stew Pet Food
The Honest Kitchen Pet food
Wysong Pet Food
Complete Natural Nutrition Pet Treats
Solid Gold Pet Food
Dogswell Pet Food
Dr. Harvey's Pet Food
Fromm Family Pet Foods
Red Bard Pet Products
Canine caviar Pet Foods
Kumpi Pet Foods
Raw Health Pet Food
Champion (Origen and Acana) Pet Foods

Pet Food Personal Experience - Tristan

I remember the day I brought him home. The breeders had given me some food to take home with me and I went out that night to get some puppy food to mix with it in order to gradually wean him off of the breeder's food. Changing food abruptly causes a lot of problems with dogs and I knew it was best to find one brand and stick with it. Especially colllies - they seem to have more sensitive stomachs than with other breeds.

I don't remember who exactly recommended Nutro Lamb and Rice to me, but it was someone whose opinion I respected and I bought the bag to bring home. As Tristan got older we of course switched to Adult dog food and stayed with the same brand. I thought I was feeding him well.

My experience with Colties has always been that they can be rather finicky with food and I found Tristan to be no exception. He would turn his nose up at his kibble many times but eat it the next day. I THOUGHT this was a good brand of food so I didn't cater to his supposedly finicky ways. My other dog, a Jack Russell, would gobble the food up so I really didn't think it was the brand that was the problem.

Over Tristan's entire life, I don't think he ate his food three days in a row. The morning routine before work was choreographed to perfection. I gave him enough time to decide whether or not he was going to eat that day and then if it wasn't consumed, I put the food up for the next day. This prevented my Jack Russell from eating it. When Tristan became hungry enough - he would eat. I always thought he had enough to eat - I always thought he just didn't have a good appetite. Again, my Jack Russell was gobbling the stuff up every day, so I didn't think anything was wrong.

When Tristan was 10 years old, a very odd thing happened. My dogs had ALWAYS been taught to leave human food alone. Collies especially can be trained NEVER to jump on a table or to snatch food from a countertop. That kind of training is embedded in their personalities, and they go to great lengths not to displease. But one day I came home and found my dog on top on the kitchen table eating the Christmas goose that was left out from the night before! I didn't know WHAT to think and immediately got a broom and swooshed him off the table. Tristan turned to me, bared his teeth, and growled a very low guttural growl. I was SHOCKED! This was beyond anything he had ever done before and it took a good 15 minutes before he stopped growling at me. Finally recognition started creeping back into his eyes and he became once again, the loving dog I had always known. He even seemed somewhat embarrassed about the incident and tried very hard to ask my forgiveness. We spent that night curled up together on the bed. I was crying very hard. This threatening, aggressive creature was not my wonderful collie. He was NOT the dog who loved us and would do anything he could to be the perfect pet.

I was worried - I went to the vet the next day and discussed options. The vet said that such marked diversions from a normal personality could be attributed to many things - a brain tumor, a stroke, etc. But it wasn't normal. I decided to put him down. The aggressiveness was too frightening and there were no guarantees that it wouldn't happen again. I had a child to think of and it was one of the hardest decisions I have ever made. My son grew up with this dog, he was a part of our lives and we loved him with all our hearts.

Several months later I decided it was time to get another collie. I know from experience that a new dog doesn't replace the one you lose, but it fills the hole in your heart. The breeder had a young male available and I jumped at the chance to take him. So Corbin came into our lives.

196

Again - I weaned him off the breeders food and started him on a Nutro Lamb and Rice kibble. A funny thing happened. Corbin started exhibiting the same exact eating behaviors that Tristan had! He wouldn't touch his food some days, and then when hungry enough, he would finally eat. This dog went from having a good appetite (on the breeder's food) to being very finicky about eating the Nutro. This time however, I couldn't dismiss it as a picky appetite. Corbin was a young adult who had no problems with appetite - it HAD to be the food!!!

I switched foods and have not had ONE problem with the dogs not eating. Corbin eats his kibble every day and would ask for more if he could.

So a lot of things have been going through my mind. Could Tristan's odd behavior been attributed to poor nutrition? 10 years is a good life span for a collie but it is not indicative of a well nourished collie. My Jack Russell died a couple of years later at the age of 13. Again, it is a good life span for a Jack Russell but not indicative of a well nourished Jack Russell.

If a dog dislikes a food so much that they are willing to starve themselves - then something isn't right. I have since learned that there is a HUGE difference in the quality of dog foods. I will NEVER EVER make that mistake again.

Phyllis B.

What you can do in case of a Pet Death or Illness

Using a "back door" tactic that worked!

Your pet gets sick from what you believe was directly caused by a pet food, treat, or other pet product. You have a $2000 vet bill to pay, (hopefully) a recovering pet, and an uninterested pet food (pet product) manufacturer. Where can you turn to advocate for your pet and be reimbursed for expenses? The answer is Small Claims Court armed with excellent documentation of the event. Going in the back door to recover costs and hold the manufacturer accountable WORKS!

As unfair and heartbreaking as it is, pets get sick and often die from a pet food, a pet treat, or other pet product that is NOT related to any recall. The FDA has established a new "*Safety Reporting Portal*," but the FDA does not provide pet owners with the number of adverse events reported that are directly related to pet food or pet treats, nor do we know which pet products are being reported to the federal agency. And, of course, no pet food or pet treat company ever provides petsumers with information of adverse event reporting.

I learn of two or three sick pets each week. ConsumerAffair.com, a website that allows consumers/petsumers to post adverse event instances, receives dozens of pet product-related reports each week. Everything from vomiting, diarrhea, and refusing to eat, to serious liver or kidney disease is being reported to veterinarians with pet owner suspicion directly relating the incident to a pet food, treat, or pet product each week. We can conservatively estimate that hundreds of pets become sick and/or die directly related to a pet food, pet treat, or other pet product each week. For those of you who have been in these shoes, you know where I'm heading next. When the panic subsides, the madness begins. Will my pet survive? Are other pets getting sick? What do I do now? Who do I call? Will I be reimbursed for my vet bills? And you will think of many more questions.

Many pet owners become angry and justifiably so. When a pet owner has just experienced a pet's suffering or even dying from an adverse reaction to a pet food, treat, or pet product, they want answers. If vet bills were incurred, or, horribly, if the pet dies, they want accountability. And then the madness gets worse.

Just try finding a lawyer who will represent you to recover thousands of dollars in vet bills. It's close to impossible! For starters, the legal system does not recognize pets as anything of value. Legally, they are no more important or valuable than, say, your couch. Next, imagine the resources it would take for a law firm to go up against a mega corporation such as Mars Petcare (Nutro, Pedigree, Royal Canin) or Nestle (Purina) or Colgate Palmolive (Science Diet). Even in the case of a pet death, you'll be hard pressed to find a law firm willing to help you take on a pet food company for damages.

While some pet food/treat companies are stepping up and offering to pay for veterinary expenses if sufficient proof is provided, many times they don't bother. Some don't even bother to return your calls or emails. "*They*" know you probably don't have documented evidence and "*they*" know there is not much you can do about it.

Aaaah...but there is! We just have to use the back door to accountability, Small Claims Court.

In March 2010, 72 year old dog owner Frank Bowers took the Hartz Mountain Corporation to Small Claims Court and won a $4,440.75 case. A Hartz Spot On Flea Treatment killed his dog within 35 hours of application.

ConsumerAffairs.com journalist Lisa McCormick called it a "*David-versus-Goliath court battle*." This determined pet owner with no law degree took on a Big Dog and won, a valuable lesson for all of us! (99)

So, if you find yourself in the midst of a sick pet and no accountability from the manufacturer, you must begin your Small Claims Court trek with proper documented evidence. No evidence, no case.

Dr. Gary Pusillo, animal lover and animal feed forensic scientist extraordinaire provided me with some advice for pet owners regarding proper documentation.

After reporting the incident to the FDA and to your state Department of Agriculture...

Document the purchase of the pet food completely - cost, date, and all observations before, during and after its use.

Detailed pictures of the incident are extremely important, as is preservation of the evidence. Do not give all of the food to the FDA or Dept of Agriculture. Save some in your freezer, clearly marked. Document the date and time you preserved the food. Document with name, date, and time each individual to whom you provided pet food.

Report the incident to the pet food manufacturer. Document every word - individual's name you speak with, title or position with the pet food company, date and time (length of conversation). Document if the pet food company does not return your call or respond to your email. Document each additional time you attempt to report the issue.

Document every piece of information received from your veterinarian. Ask your veterinarian to write a full statement including his/her belief as to the cause of the pet illness. Obtain copies of all test results. If you discover reports of other similar pet illnesses, obtain as much information from these pet owners as they can provide. Ask them to have their statements notarized and include their full name, address, and telephone number. (You might be asked to provide the same for them).

When/if the pet food manufacturer does not promptly agree to reimburse you for all expenses, file for your day in Small Claims Court.

Every state's Small Claims Court laws are different. Visit your County Government website to learn more about the process.

Pet owners don't have much recourse available when a pet product sickens or kills our pet. But we do have Small Claims Court. It could be that such effort by pet owners could change the safety of all pet products!

Now just think about this. Imagine if there were a dozen pet food-related Small Claims Court cases each month. Imagine if, at each Small Claims Court across the country, the pet product manufacturer had to be represented by legal counsel in order to defend its case and protect its image. Imagine this happening week after week after week, hundreds of cases, millions of dollars in legal fees incurred by pet product manufacturers …and no legal fees paid by the pet owner since you will be proudly representing yourself and your pet! I'm fairly confident "*they*" will sit up and take notice. Remember, a 72 year old pet owner took his very difficult case to Small Claims Court and won. You can, too.

Do your homework, be brave, and hold them accountable!

In Case of Illness Related to Pet Food

Are you prepared should a pet food make your pet sick? What to do and not do should your dog or cat become ill from a pet food is addressed here.

I hear from thousands of pet owners with sick pets. These pet owners are confident a pet food is the cause of their pets' death or illness. Sadly, these instances of possible pet food contamination cannot be investigated because the pet owners were not aware that they needed to keep the batch numbers found on the pet food label. Without batch numbers, the FDA cannot investigate the food. It doesn't seem fair, especially if you have lost a pet or are treating a sick pet, but this is how it is with the FDA.

The lesson for all of us to remember is to keep your pet food bag or can label until you are certain your pet is ok.

Many pet owners empty their bag of kibble dog food or cat food into an airtight bin after opening. While I encourage this, since the airtight bin helps keep the food fresh, without information from the bag or can no investigation will be done.

With canned foods, tear the label off the can and keep it handy for at least a few days to a few weeks after it was consumed. Just in case the canned food causes your pet to become ill, you, the pet food company, and the FDA will have batch numbers to investigate.

With kibble foods, keep the bag until your pet has finished the entire bag without incident.

Just a reminder...
Know what normal behavior is for your pet, especially normal eating habits and normal elimination habits. Any variation of "*normal*" could be your first sign of a health problem, whether food related or non-food related.

Closely examine the outside of the bag or can before you purchase. Do not purchase any dog food or cat food that has tears, stains, or dents (cans). Closely examine the food when you open the bag or can. It should look and smell exactly like the previous purchase. If it does not, do not feed it to your pet. Return it to the store for a refund.

If your pet is standoffish or suddenly picky with the food, stop feeding the food immediately. Oftentimes our pets "*tell*" us when something is wrong with the food. Listen to what they are telling you.

Keep the bag or can labels for at least several days to several weeks after your pet has consumed the food so that the food can be identified and investigated.

Should your pet become ill, consult your veterinarian immediately. Ask your veterinarian to report the illness as possibly food related to the FDA. You (the pet owner) should report the issue to the pet food company, the FDA, and to your state Department of Agriculture. This webpage is a list of FDA coordinators for each state: http://www.fda.gov/Safety/ ReportaProblem/ConsumerComplaintCoordinators/default.htm

Have a back-up pet food ready...
"*Things*" do happen. Being prepared for those "*things*" could make a huge difference for your pet and your stress level. One major preparation is having a small bag of back-up pet food in your freezer or several cans stored in your pantry. This back-up food should be a completely different brand than your "*regular*" pet food in case the entire line is tainted.

Your back-up food should contain similar ingredients as your "*regular*" dog food or cat food. As an example, if your regular pet food uses chicken meal as the main meat protein, your back-up pet food should use chicken meal as well. Make sure the back-up food contains probiotics, just like your regular food, chelated minerals and similar health-promoting ingredients. Changing foods quickly is not much of an issue with cats, but it can be for dogs. Keeping ingredients as close as possible with your back-up food could help to prevent tummy issues should you have to use it. Cats can get "*stuck*" on kibble size and shape and become finicky when changing foods.

Keep your back-up kibble food stored in your freezer, not on a shelf in the pantry. The freezer storage will keep it fresh. Every six months replace the old back-up bag of dog food or cat food with a new bag. Use or discard the old bag.

Canned back-up pet food can be stored in the pantry since most canned foods remain fresh for 2+ years. However, I would change back-up canned food once a year.

Another option is to rotate your pets' food once a month or so. Have two or three different pet foods you like and trust and change your pet to a new food in the rotation the beginning of every month. Most dogs need to change food slowly - ¼ new food to ¾ old food for several days, ½ to ½ for several days, and so on. Dogs that have sensitive tummies need to change foods even more slowly. Cats can typically change foods immediately.

If you rotate foods, store the next food in the rotation in your freezer (kibble) and it can/could be used as a back up food if you have a problem with the food you are currently using.

Vindication

Pet owners are nothing short of amazing. Although many pet owners' lives have been shattered by pet food, and although the pet food industry itself has not been kind to pet owners in their grief, pet owners continue to fight the fight for safe pet food. Vindication helps to ease the pain, if even just a little.

Losing your dog or cat because a pet food was contaminated is one of the worst experiences a pet owner can endure. You feel guilty. You feel taken advantage of. You feel lied to. You feel alone. The most unbelievable levels of anger and guilt churn in your gut. BECAUSE OF A PET FOOD...many have held their dear friend for the last time while a lethal drug is injected into their body to end their pain and end their life. BECAUSE OF A PET FOOD...countless others have suffered right alongside their pet holding on to the hope that they recover. Watching them die is haunting. BECAUSE OF A PET FOOD...thousands more continue to nurse their bodies damaged by pet food day in and day out. It is the worst emotional roller coaster ride imaginable. The vet bills have maxed out your credit cards. Your pet-less friends look at you like you've gone off the deep end, the pet food company investigation will be

It happened six times to one family. They have buried six pets because of pet food in the 2007 recall, four cats and two dogs.

Here is their story of Zippy, just one of thousands of beloved pets that pet food has killed:

He was a stillborn baby kitten. His human mom puffed the first tiny breath into his lungs and massaged his heart. She felt its first beat.

Zippy was not a typical cat. He was more of a clumsy comedian. Seems he couldn't make it across a carpeted floor without tumbling to the ground once or twice. A toe nail always tangled him up in carpeting. Day in and day out, the ceiling fan startled him. He was best friends with a cockatiel. He didn't know birds and cats weren't supposed to be friends. It is a family joke that Zippy wasn't the brightest bulb in the box, but he was loved, so loved, by his human family.

Zippy's sister was one of the first that died. For two years, Zippy continued to search and cry for his poisoned sister. For two years, Zippy became sicker and sicker from the ravages of melamine-laced pet food. The damage was done. His human mom had felt his heart's first beat under her fingertip and she felt his heart's last beat when she was forced to euthanize his failing body.

One shattered pet family decided enough was enough. These courageous pet owners donated five acres of land at Keystone Lake near Tulsa, Oklahoma for a pet memorial and named it Vindication. It was created to remember pets that died or that remain ill due to a contaminated pet food or treat. Each and every pet name submitted is remembered in Vindication with its own handmade pathway stone.

Vindication is being sculpted by the donors into flowering gardens with handmade stones lining the cascading pathways. A careful selection of flowers will bloom both day and night. At the very front of the land will be 16 handmade stones circled into the pathway beginning. These 16 stones signify the 16 "official" pets that died at the Menu Foods testing laboratory long before the deadliest recall in world history was announced. Each innocent victim is remembered. Thousands of pets will be honored here. Vindication will even include a Rainbow Bridge.

Every pet owner who has lost a pet due to a pet food or treat and every pet owner who still cares for a pet sick from a pet food or treat is welcome to submit their pet's name to be honored in Vindication. Visit TruthaboutPetFood.com and click on the Vindication banner to register your pet.

Plans are for Vindication to be open to the public in the summer of 2011. A day which will celebrate the memory of our beloved lost friends and those who continue to struggle.

These pets….nor the reason they died…. will ever be forgotten.

"One of the unspoken truths of American life is how deeply people grieve over animals who live and die with them, how real the emptiness is, how profound is the silence these creatures leave in their wake."
From Dog Years by Mark Doty

Lastly...

I wish I could tell you there is a perfect pet food; a pet food that will never be recalled made by a company that will always take every precaution and use only the finest of ingredients. I can't tell you that.

I do not recommend or endorse any pet food. However, I firmly believe there are many pet food companies that search for the finest suppliers of ingredients, test those ingredients with each batch, and closely monitor the manufacturing process. Finding who those pet food companies are is easier said than done. As you've learned from this book, pet food regulatory authorities do not have the best interest of the pet food consumer in mind.

The best advice I can give you is to do a little homework before you buy that bag or can of pet food. Re-read the Do's and Don'ts chapter of this book. Call the pet food manufacturer and get the answers you need. If they do not respond promptly and provide you with complete answers, don't buy their product. Examine every bag or can before you open it and after you open it. If anything looks or smells different, don't give it to your pet. And always 'listen' to your pet. Know what is normal behavior (eating, activity, elimination); any variation from normal behavior could be a signal of a health problem. Consult with your veterinarian if your pet alters from normal behavior.

If you change pet foods, change slowly (especially for dogs). It is recommended to add 1/4 new food to 3/4 old food for four to five days, 1/2 to 1/2 for another four to five days, and so on. Some pets (again mostly for dogs) have to change even slower than this. If your new pet food contains probiotics, you might notice your pet having some gas. It takes a couple of weeks for the 'tummy' to get used to probiotics.

And for cat owners, please give them wet/canned food. Leading experts in cat nutrition have proven the tremendous benefit of wet food to cats. For more information, visit Dr. Lisa Pierson DVM's website www.catinfo.org.

Lastly...

As for my pets, what do they eat? They eat home cookin'.

About the Author

I joke that I am an 'Ellie Mae Clampet' (if you are old enough to remember the TV show The Beverly Hillbillies); critters have always been a big part of my life. My first dog as a child was a red Doberman named Duke. My grandfather used to take me to obedience classes each week, and I competed with Duke in obedience trials. Back then, it was standard to teach dogs using force (do this or I'll hurt you methods). Even at 11 years old, and in defiance of those who were teaching me 'how to train my dog', I refused to hurt my best friend. My kind methods of training paid off, out of a possible 200 points, we consistently scored 199 and 199 1/2 in competitions. Duke was my best friend and he was treated with respect; he returned the favor ten fold.

At 15, my parents bought me a horse for my birthday. I went from showing dogs to showing horses. And yes, Duke went to the barn with me almost every day. My respect of animals continued with my horses; I had the number one Quarter Horse gelding (neutered male horse) in the State of Kentucky for several years. I went to college on a horsemanship scholarship; taking three horses with me to school. A good friend teases me that 'normal' girls go to college with three hair dryers, I preferred three horses.

Down the road a few years, at 27 years old, I started my own business, The Pet School in Louisville, KY. The Pet School was a dog obedience school that did things differently; I taught basic obedience lessons to spoiled rotten house pets. The very same kind and respectful methods I used to train my own pets. Needless to say, there were many other pet owners who wanted to treat their dogs respectfully in training.

Within a few years I added a boarding kennel to my business. Using the same logic I always had with my animals, I wanted a kennel to be different than what was offered at the time; a facility that kept the dogs and cats safe, but that was as close to home as possible. I'm proud to say that my kennel was the very first all indoor/all suite pet boarding facility in the U.S. Every 'room' had a window, and every pet got to play each day during their stay.

My number one assistant, was Sam, a female spoiled rotten Rottweiler.

I've been blessed with many special animals in my life, Sam was one of the extra special dogs. She was commonly a headrest for my children growing up; she even helped them learn to walk. And, she worked with me every day, being the 'demo' dog in all my obedience classes. She had a sense of which dogs were intimidated; she'd wiggle over to them and kiss them to calm their fears. Alternatively, if another dog attempted to be a little bossy with their classmates, she quickly let them know she was top dog in the classroom.

When Sam was eight years old, I noticed a lump on her pelvic area. A trip to my trusted Veterinarian showed it was bone cancer; I had two weeks to tell her good-bye. The worst news was the veterinarian I had known and trusted since I was a child, told me the probable cause of Sam's cancer was from the chemical preservatives in her food. The food that I gave her.

I couldn't believe what my veterinarian, Dr. Bruce Catlett, was telling me. This dog food was the number one pet food in the U.S.; it was a 'trusted' company. What I did next changed me forever.

Dr. Catlett told me that these chemical preservatives were (and still are) added to pet foods to extend their 'shelf life'; to keep them fresh for longer periods of time for retail purposes. I called the pet food company; I asked them what the shelf life was on this food. I'll never forget it - they told me the shelf life was "*25 years*". That's more than three times as long as my dog lived.

The chemical that killed Sam - was ethoxyquin; it is still commonly used in many dog foods, cat foods, and pet treats. The pet food company that killed her, is still one of the top pet food companies; although they no longer use ethoxyquin in their foods, they use many other disease causing ingredients including dangerous chemicals.

Dr. Catlett came to my home and put Sam down. I dug her grave. Her most favorite thing to do was play ball. She had a ball in her mouth when she took her last breath; and she was buried with it.

Sam's death changed me forever. From that day forward, I have studied pet foods, pet food ingredients, and the regulations that govern them.

Today I'm known as the 'Caped Crusader for Safe Pet Food' (a title given to me by a dear friend); regulatory authorities, Big Pet Food, Veterinarians, and a world of pet owners follow my website. I was invited to speak at a Veterinary School and have been denied admission to pet food trade events (were they afraid of what I'd learn?). None of this would have happened without a world of support from pet owners. TruthaboutPetFood.com is really a team of pet owners sick that (some) commercial pet food continues to kill pets.

Just like so many pet owners, I learned the 'truth' about pet foods the hard way. The purpose of this book and my website TruthaboutPet-Food.com is to help prevent other Pet Owners from learning the hard way what some pet foods contain. The website continues to publish pet food educational articles and news updates about the pet food industry. Myself and a team of pet lovers continue to fight illegal pet food regulations. Please visit TruthaboutPetFood.com and register for the free newsletter to stay updated.

(1) http://www.thehonestkitchen.com/2007/11/08/fresh-news/

(2) http://www.fda.gov/RegulatoryInformation/Legislation/FederalFood
DrugandCosmeticActFDCAct/FDCActChapterIVFood/default.htm

(3) http://www.fda.gov/ICECI/ComplianceManuals/CompliancePolicy
GuidanceManual/UCM074717

(4) http://www.fws.gov/mountain-prairie/poison.pdf

(5) http://www.fda.gov/ICECI/ComplianceManuals/CompliancePolicy
GuidanceManual/ucm074693.htm

(6) http://www.fda.gov/ICECI/ComplianceManuals/CompliancePolicy
GuidanceManual/ucm074694.htm

(7) http://www.fda.gov/ICECI/EnforcementActions/WarningLetters/ucm
224571.htm

(8) http://www.fda.gov/ICECI/ComplianceManuals/CompliancePolicy
GuidanceManual/UCM074717)

(9) http://www.fda.gov/cvm/AFSS051408Welcome.htm

(10) http://www.fda.gov/cvm/AFSSprojplan5.htm

(11) http://www.consumeraffairs.com/news04/2009/04/nutro_foia.html

(12) http://www.truthaboutpetfood.com/articles/toxic-levels-of-vitamin-d-found-in-
nutro-cat-food.html

(13) http://www.fda.gov/AdvisoryCommittees/CommitteesMeetingMaterials/
ScienceBoardtotheFoodandDrugAdministration/ucm115370.htm

(14) http://www.nih.gov/news/health/oct2008/niddk-08.htm

(15) http://online.wsj.com/article/SB122400110147832865.html?mod=google
news_wsj

(16) http://www.etaiwannews.com/etn/news_content.php?id=765092

(17) http://www.cbsnews.com/8301-504763_162-20010219-10391704.html

(18) http://www.wisconsinagconnection.com/story-national.php?Id=1374&yr=2010

(19) http://ntp.niehs.nih.gov/files/9MelamineGGCosta.pdf

(20) http://www.newsweek.com/id/232962/page/2

(21) http://www.truthaboutpetfood.com/articles/world%E2%80%99s-top-five-pet-food-producers-in-retail-sales.html

(22) http://www.commondreams.org/headlines02/0106-02.htm

(23) http://www.citypaper.com/about/vansmith.asp

(24) http://www.commondreams.org/headlines02/0106-04.htm

(25) http://www.fda.gov/oc/opacom/hottopics/bse.html

(26) http://www.fsis.usda.gov...

(27) http://www.fda.gov/cvm/FOI/DFreport.htm

(28) http://www.fda.gov/AboutFDA/CentersOffices/CVM/CVMFOIAElectronic ReadingRoom/ucm129135.htm

(29) http://www.fda.gov/AboutFDA/CentersOffices/CVM/CVMFOIAElectronic ReadingRoom/ucm129131.htm

(30) http://www.fda.gov/AnimalVeterinary/NewsEvents/FDAVeterinarian Newsletter/ucm093929.htm

(31) http://www.aseanfood.info/Articles/11021372.pdf

(32) http://www.westonaprice.org/know-your-fats/559-the-great-con-ola.html

(33) http://www.dldewey.com/columns/canola.htm

(34) http://www.epa.gov/pesticides/biopesticides/ingredients/index_cd.htm#c

(35) http://www.cfsan.fda.gov/~dms/qhccanol.html

(36) http://www.jacn.org/cgi/content/full/20/suppl_5/417S

(37) http://www.sciencedirect.com/science?_ob=ArticleURL&_udi=B6TCN-484VG15-4&_user=10&_coverDate=05%2F03%2F2003&_rdoc=1&_fmt=high&_orig=search&_sort=d&_docanchor=&view=c&_searchStrId=1428856463&_rerunOrigin=google&_acct=C000050221&_version=1&_urlVersion=0&_userid=10&md5=47401745d749da5d3f007f6c69250d99

(38) http://jn.nutrition.org/cgi/content/full/134/6/1347

(39) http://truefoodnow.org/about/

(40) http://www.ncbi.nlm.nih.gov/pmc/articles/PMC2793308/?log%24=activity

(41) http://www.anh-usa.org/urgent-action-alert-tell-fda-to-ban-arsenic-in-animal-feed/

(42) http://www.iatp.org/iatp/publications.cfm?accountID=421&refID=80529

(43) http://www.petfoodindustry.com/ViewArticle.aspx?id=12892#Scene_1

(44) http://www.chemicalbook.com/CASEN_91-53-2.htm

(45) http://www.epa.gov/oppsrrd1/REDs/factsheets/0003fact.pdf

(46) http://www.chemicalbook.com/ChemicalProductProperty_EN_CB5296077.htm

(47) http://www.fda.gov/animalveterinary/resourcesforyou/ucm047113.htm

(48) http://en.wikipedia.org/wiki/Propylene_glycol#Animals

(49) http://www.sefsc.noaa.gov/HTMLdocs/PropyleneGlycol.htm

(50) http://www.cosmeticsdatabase.com/ingredient.php?ingred06=705315

(51) http://recipes.howstuffworks.com/question315.htm (this link includes an interesting video on harvesting carrageenan.)

(52) http://www.ncbi.nlm.nih.gov/pmc/articles/PMC1242073/

(53) http://monographs.iarc.fr/ENG/Classification/Listagentsalphorder.pdf

(54) http://www.internet-grocer.net/realmeat.htm

(55) http://www.ewg.org/node/28070

(56) http://en.wikipedia.org/wiki/Canning

(57) http://www.hsph.harvard.edu/news/press-releases/2009-releases/bpa-chemical-plastics-leach-polycarbonate-drinking-bottles-humans.html

(58) http://www.jacn.org/cgi/content/full/20/1/1

(59) http://www.nutriteck.com/bulk/selenium.html

(60) http://www.eco-usa.net/toxics/selenium.shtml

(61) http://www.sciencelab.com/msds.php?msdsId=9927277

(62) http://www.ncbi.nlm.nih.gov/pubmed/15522125

(63) http://www.sciencelab.com/xMSDS-Menadione sodium bisulfite-9924604

(64) http://digital.findanalytichem.com/nxtbooks/advanstar/spectroscopy0111_v2/index.php#/48

(66) http://www.equidblog.com/uploads/file/probiotics.pdf

(67) http://www.wasamedicals.com/pdf/ref_smj_eng.pdf

(68) http://jn.nutrition.org/cgi/content/full/130/2/415S

(69) http://www.ncbi.nlm.nih.gov/pmc/articles/PMC340078/

(70) http://www.ncbi.nlm.nih.gov/pmc/articles/PMC340366/

(71) http://www.avma.org/press/releases/100304_omega-3_fatty_acids.asp

(72) http://avmajournals.avma.org/doi/abs/10.2460/javma.236.1.67?prevSearch=allfield%253A%2528Hahn%2529&searchHistoryKey=

(73) http://avmajournals.avma.org/doi/abs/10.2460/javma.236.1.59?prevSearch=allfield%253A%2528Hahn%2529&searchHistoryKey=

(74) http://avmajournals.avma.org/doi/abs/10.2460/javma.236.5.535?
prevSearch=allfield%253A%2528Hahn%2529&searchHistoryKey=

(75) http://www.fda.gov/NewsEvents/Newsroom/PressAnnouncements/
2008/ucm116915.htm

(76) http://www.nytimes.com/2010/03/15/business/media/15
adnewsletter1.html?pagewanted=2

(77) http://www.naturalnews.com/029291_cancer_diet.html

(78) http://live.ift.org/2010/07/19/healthier-pets-make-for-healthier-people/

(79) http://www.blackwell-synergy.com/doi/abs/10.1111/j.1748-5827.2008.00589.x

(79) http://www.oprah.com/article/oprahandfriends/moz/20080602_
oaf_moz_amazingomega3s

(80) http://www.zonediet.com/OMEGA3/tabid/64/Default.aspx

(81) http://www.mcneilproductrecall.com/page.jhtml?id=/include/press.inc

(82) http://www.fda.gov/ICECI/ComplianceManuals/CompliancePolicy
GuidanceManual/ucm074710.htm

(83) http://www.msnbc.msn.com/id/38851155/ns/health-food_safety/

(84) http://pediatrics.aappublications.org/cgi/content/abstract/peds.2009-3273v1

(85) http://www.petcare.mars.com/default.html

(86) http://www.cdc.gov/mmwr/preview/mmwrhtml/mm5744a2.htm

(87) http://www.associatedcontent.com/article/1034410/pedigree_issues_
national_pet_food_recall.html?cat=3

(88) http://www.accessdata.fda.gov/scripts/newpetfoodrecalls/

(89) http://www.accessdata.fda.gov/scripts/HVPCP/

(90) http://efoodalert.blogspot.com/2010/08/fda-focus-on-pet-products-
stimulates.html

(91) http://www.accessdata.fda.gov/scripts/HVPCP/

(92) http://abcnews.go.com/Health/Wellness/dry-pet-food-linked-salmonella-children/story?id=11344300

(93) http://consumerist.com/consumer/complaints/petco-sells-dog-food-that-expired-3-years-ago-312921.php

(94) http://www.sustainabletable.org/issues/irradiation/

(95) http://www.petconnection.com/blog/2009/10/22/wysong-pet-food-recall-way-to-miss-the-point/

(96) http://www.truthaboutpetfood.com/articles/473/1/Statement-from-Wysong-Pet-Foods/Page1.html

(97) http://www.fda.gov/ForConsumers/ConsumerUpdates/ucm049070.htm

(98) http://www.truthaboutpetfood.com/articles/more-on-ethoxyquin-preserved-fish-meals.html

(99) http://www.consumeraffairs.com/news04/2010/03/hartz_mountain_court.html